To Stephanie, Zachary, and Mackenzie.

'Never bend your head. Always hold it high.
Look the world straight in the eye.'

Live fearlessly. Risk boldly. Trust God unashamedly.
Face every giant with courage and reckless abandon to Jesus.
Go passionately after your God-inspired dreams.
I hope you dance!

I'm honored to be your father.

Table of Contents

Acknowledgements

Life wouldn't be worth the journey without having the right people around you. I'm grateful for all of you.

First and foremost, I am indebted to Jesus Christ for his amazing grace in my life. The pages of this book would be blank if not for his redemptive passion, substitutionary death on the cross, and life-giving resurrection.

Cindy, thank you for teaching me all about love, life, and laughter. It's been a wonderful ride for fifteen years now. Our best days are ahead of us!

Stephanie, Zachary, and Mackenzie, you give me more than enough sermon illustrations for a lifetime. I love telling the stories of your lives.

Mom, you've faced enormous giants in your life and have overcome. Thank you for your inspiration. Bob ("Pop-Pop"), thank you for becoming the father I never had growing up. You've given our family enduring strength. Your character-based leadership is unparalleled. I wish every family had a father like you in their home. Society would look much different.

Bob and Terri, you are the best in-laws in the world. I love you dearly. You wrote the book on parenting, rearing the most virtuous woman alive.

Anne Ruth Hicks, your legacy of love continues in all of our hearts.

Charlie, Patti, and Myra, thank you for the gift of family.

Reverend Alan "Preacher" Woody, thank you for being a faithful servant of Christ. You not only taught me what it means to live by faith, you modeled it.

Jarrod Pillsbury, your friendship has meant more than you will ever know. I hope, for your sake, there is a Taco Bell in heaven.

Ross and Debbie Hoffmeier, if everyone in this world had your hearts, there'd be no hurting kids!

Our world changers with Breakaway Outreach, there is no greater cause on earth than reaching the next generation with the Gospel and empowering them to face their giants. We have much work to do!

Introduction

On September 10th, 1987, I sat in a cold, roach-infested cell of a juvenile detention center reflecting over the sixteen years of my life, which at the time felt more like fifty years. I had been locked up for three days now, spending the bulk of them observing every doorway, barbed-wire fence, barred window, and crevice, looking for a possible means to escape. I had grown accustomed to running. As a matter of fact, running is what ultimately landed me in the juvie center in the first place.

Just one year earlier I had attempted suicide and spent four days in the ICU at a hospital in Baltimore. I didn't necessarily want to die, I just didn't see any real reason to be alive or any hope in being delivered from the inhuman abuses of my father. To understand how my life had come to such a dismal resolve you must know where it all began.

It has taken me over 25 years to publish the injustices that were a part of my childhood, yet the events are as clear to me today as if they had happened yesterday. Some of these events were so painful to address, insomuch that I would much rather intentionally leave them in the past where they are nestled far away from the joys I experience with my wonderful family today. But frankly, that would be too *safe*. And because God never intends to waste our pain or suffering, I choose to obey Him in sharing my story with the hope that it will bring about healing for victims of abuse everywhere, even if it makes me feel dangerously vulnerable.

Humanity is a messy place to learn how to become fully alive. Nevertheless, it is indeed a boot camp of faith; a spiritual gauntlet in which God calls every one of us to go through if we are to bear the resemblance of His Son, Jesus. And I've learned over the years that pain is not only an unfortunate part of this growth process; it is indeed a very necessary, vital, and essential part of our journey. My hope is that as you read this book you will come to experience the same grace I've experienced in discovering God's redemptive purpose through pain and suffering, and to have the perfect peace that even when our pain doesn't make sense, our heavenly Father's love remains steadfast.

His love can be *trusted* even when a "Why" cannot be *traced*.

13-Foot Coffins is not necessarily my story, it's His-story; one where I have been given the humble privilege of being an *extra* that points to the main character in this story: Jesus Christ. This account is a living chronicle of God's redemptive work in a fallen world where generational curses run rampant, and specifically, His intimate dealings in rescuing a helpless child out of the cruelty of injustice and the despair of abuse, to setting him free from a victim mentality, to becoming a difference maker in giving hope to countless young people across the globe. I am no longer a *victim*; I am more than a *conqueror* through HIM who loved me out of darkness and into His glorious light (Romans 8:37). Healing, forgiveness, and freedom can be found for those who truly want to become fully alive.

Welcome to His story; one in which I serve as a humble stagehand in lifting up the unbound Healer, faithful Redeemer, and Prince of Peace: Jesus, the risen Christ!

Join me in this rich journey of grace in slaying a victim-mentality and finding your God-inspired dance with destiny!

The world is waiting.

Chapter One
Giants Were Meant to be Slain

*The story of your life is the story of the journey of your heart through
a dangerous and beautiful world. It is the story of the long and
sustained assault on your heart by the Enemy who knows who you
could be... and fears you.*
~ John Eldredge

Major Richard D. Winters is a former United States Army officer and decorated war veteran. He commanded *Easy Company*, 2nd Battalion, 506th Parachute Infantry Regiment, and the 101st Airborne Division during World War II. His admirable service was chronicled in the 2001 HBO mini-series *Band of Brothers*.

In the closing segments of the series' fifth episode, after Company "E" gets a rare weekend pass and siesta in Paris, news arrives of a massive Axis effort in the Ardennes Forest, threatening to break the Allied lines. The unparalleled confrontation to come would later become known as the Battle of the Bulge, Germany's last major offensive launched toward the end of World War II. Easy Company races in to hold the line, ill-equipped for the bitterly cold weather and the entrenched battle ahead. As the troops move into position, they pass by a retreating division of "green" America soldiers that have been shell-shocked and pummeled by the enemy.

The outgoing Lt. George Rice says to the incoming Major Winters, "Panzer division is about to cut the road south. Looks like you guys are going to be surrounded." Winters calmly, yet confidently assures Rice, "We're paratroopers, Lieutenant. We're supposed to be surrounded."

As the episode ends and fades to black, a graphic tells us that Easy moved into the Bastogne woods without support from the sky or from artillery, and that they lacked food, ammunition, and winter clothes. Then this quote from the 506th Parachute Infantry Regiment's "Currahee Scrapbook" appears on the screen: "Farthest from your mind is the thought of falling back; in fact, it isn't there at all. And so you dig your hole carefully and deep, and wait."

I don't know where you find yourself right now and what circumstances surround your life. But I can tell you this: you are supposed to be surrounded. It's the nature of who you are and what God has called you to do in this world. And unless you want to forfeit your dance with destiny, retreating is not an option. But you must also be reassured that he who is in you is greater than he who is in the world (1 John 4:4). *You were meant to overcome!*

Have you ever wondered why the stories and films that seem to resonate most with our hearts are those with an apparent villain invading the storyline of some epic adventure? The plots that grip the hem of our hearts and seize our interest most are those with a so-called "bad guy" standing between an unlikely hero and his or her dance with destiny.

Could this intrigue be due to the belief that our story also has a villain in it?

The movies we cherish are those where good triumphs over evil, justice overcomes injustice, courage confronts the oppressor, and the underdog rises above some impossible challenge to accomplish the unthinkable. The superheroes we marvel all have their own personal archenemies. All great stories have something in common – an epic journey of adventure, beauty, and heroism – all fiercely opposed by an exasperating nemesis. The story of your life is likely no different.

Superman has his Lex Luthor.

Batman has his Joker.

David has his Goliath.

Think about the classics you read as a child: *Cinderella's* story isn't the same without her nefarious stepmother and a double dose of wicked stepsisters to demean her sense of worth, beauty, and charm. We all know what becomes of the queen's rage when she hears the words from her magical mirror: "Snow White is fairer than you." *Snow White* didn't ask for a villain, but because of her beauty and the uniqueness of her story, she found herself facing a seething giant of jealousy. In order to survive in their dog-eat-dog world, the three little pigs must find the safeguard of community to endure the ravenous appetite of the big bad wolf. *Little Red Riding Hood* must face a villain also; perhaps it was the same hungry wolf that couldn't extract the ham sandwich from the three pigs.

Moses must stand before the most powerful political and military leader of his day, defy the Pharaoh's ensuing wrath that will be unleashed upon his already subjugated people, and demand that the slaves be set free. He is a man on a dance with destiny, but things get worse before they get better. His villain ensures this.

Luke Skywalker must resist the rage of Darth Vader and the evil forces of the dark side only to discover that he is biologically related to the dark side. Talk about awkwardness at Thanksgiving get-togethers and family reunions!

Frodo and his loyal protectors have the emissaries of the Dark Lord Sauron to oppose them in their journey to save middle earth, and the closer they get to fulfilling their mission the more intense the warfare gets.

Would Peter Pan's voyage to the island of *Neverland* be as resounding with our hearts if it didn't have his arch nemesis Captain Hook constantly impeding the daring adventures of Pan and his youthful comrades?

We all remember the 1997 blockbuster *Titanic*, in which Rose must rise above the greed of her mother's materialistic compulsion and the domineering control of an abusive fiancé to discover the spirit of adventure and vivacious beauty hidden deep within the depths of her heart.

In the 2000 film *Gladiator*, Maximus Decimus Meridius is betrayed when the Emperor's ambitious son, Commodus, murders his father and seizes the throne. Reduced to slavery, Maximus must rise through the ranks of the gladiatorial arena to face his enemy and avenge the murder of his family and his Emperor. He avows to stand before his foe one day and dance with destiny. "What we do in life echoes in eternity" becomes his mantra and the slave soon enters Rome "like a conquering hero." Maximus faces his villain.

In C.S. Lewis' Chronicles of Narnia, Peter, Susan, Edmund and Lucy Pevensie discover the land of Narnia in the back of a wardrobe and venture inside to explore. Realizing its inhabitants are at the mercy of the ruthless White Witch, they join forces with the heroic lion Aslan and set out to end the self-proclaimed queen's reign of terror. They face the villain.

Joseph's brothers play the role of villains in his story. He's betrayed by his own blood and sold into slavery because of a dream that, at first glance, seems narcissistic and self-serving. Years later it proves to be God-inspired.

The villains Jesus faced daily were clothed in religious zeal. He experienced recurrent attacks from religious zealots, false accusations from Pharisees, and betrayal by one of those closest to him; and then the sinless Son of God hangs on a criminal's cross to bear the punishment for the sins of the world. His crime: loving the unlovable and hanging out with despicable sinners, those whom the religious elite had ostracized. Jesus took the sword of grace and thrust it into the heart of a Goliath named "Religious Condemnation." He faced his giant and grace prevailed.

You get the picture. Every story that has a monumental purpose and an enduring legacy also has some sort of villain in it.

The reason why all of these stories resonate with us at our deepest core is that at the center of our lives, hopes, and dreams, we also have an incensed villain who is fiercely opposed to our dance with destiny. In chapter thirteen of the Book of Revelation, we see a dramatic picture of a "beast" making war against the people of God. This beast is seen throughout Scripture, yet comes to an unprecedented climax in Revelation. Knowing his time is short, he unleashes a fury of attacks on followers of Christ in an attempt to suppress their impact on earth. Imagine it: on a daily basis you have a nemesis that is violently opposed to everything God made you to be, and is relentlessly assertive in keeping you from becoming a part of the heroic, enduring legacy that God has planned for you. He'll use betrayal, slander, fear, discouragement, anger, resentment, unforgiveness, injustice, tragedy, indifference, and even religion, to keep you from fully embracing your dance with destiny. He'll even use YOU to stifle yourself, if you let yourself become discouraged enough. Sometimes our worst enemy is the enemy "in-a-me."

Your nemesis hates you with a passion because you are a child of promise, purpose, and destiny, and you can expect all of his hordes to be unleashed against you when you begin to pursue that destiny.

You Were Made To Face Giants

Opposition.

It's not something most of us wake up every morning savoring like a cup of fresh ground Jamaican Blue coffee. Adversity doesn't come with an enchanting aroma, luring us into a state of serenity and quiescence. The truth is, we can't stand adversity. And there is something about it that gets under our skin and rattles our cages. I found this to be true even while playing Wii with my seven-year-old son. When he blocks my jump shot, the first thing I think is, "He's not supposed to be able to do that. The kid's only four feet tall." We don't like it when something stands between us and our goal; even if it is something as trivial as a video game and a forty-eight inch stature in the form of a seven-year-old blocking our jump shot. It's annoying.

The sooner we can come to grips with the fact that adversity is here to stay, the better fitted we become for our dance with destiny. And the more comfortable we get with facing adversity, the more equipped we become to respond to it.

The reason your life is so fiercely opposed is that you were made to face giants – giants of no ordinary stature… *and giants were meant to be slain.*

I can picture the early Christians gathering around a campfire one evening, beginning to question the goodness of God because of what has befallen them; hardship, persecution, physical beatings, hatred, even martyrdom for simply loving God and sharing his message with others. In some moments they must have felt lost, confused, bitterly tormented with mixed emotions of feeling abandoned by God and left to themselves in their suffering. They were human. They struggled with these emotions.

Perhaps some suggested this wasn't what they had signed up for. Others were tempted to give up… and many did. "This isn't what the TV preacher promised it would be like," cried another. We were told that if we became Christians everything would be easy… you know, we would be *safe*.

Why isn't God protecting us from danger?

Why so many hardships?

Why doesn't our faith grant us immunity to suffering?

Isn't that God's job – to keep us from danger? He's supposed to shelter us from suffering and protect us from pain… isn't He? Isn't that what Christianity has taught us? Why does the pain we are experiencing right now seem so strange, foreign, and antonymous to the theology we were taught by the "prosperity" preachers?

Enter Peter, and his admonition to the early believers:

> Beloved, do not be surprised at the fiery trial when it comes upon you to test you, as though something strange were happening to you. But rejoice insofar as you share Christ's sufferings, that you may also rejoice and be glad when his glory is revealed. (1 Peter 4:12-13 ESV)

Peter's sermons weren't going to land him a spot on Christian television anytime soon. He didn't have enough *name-it-claim-it* savvy to push prosperity books through the markets or manipulate viewers with biblical promises taken out of context. He brought the harsh, stark reality that serving Jesus would not only bring suffering, but that we should somehow find joy in it and find purpose in our pain.

After Paul was stoned and dragged out of the city of Lystra, he didn't rise up early the next day and beat himself up for not having enough faith, or claiming enough "protect-me" scriptures that could've inoculated him to suffering. He didn't commit himself to up his reading plan to thirty percent more scriptures a day. Instead, it says, "they returned to Lystra and to Iconium and to Antioch, strengthening the souls of the disciples, encouraging them to continue in the faith, and saying that *through many tribulations we must enter the kingdom of God*" (Acts 14:21-22).

Peter and Paul seemed to be in agreement with Jesus: "In the world you will have tribulation. But take heart; I have overcome the world" (John 16:33).

The early followers of Jesus ultimately found confidence in the trials they faced. They discovered we weren't meant to avoid the giants, we were meant to face giants of all sorts. You weren't made to evade the storms; you were designed to be an unsinkable vessel that goes through storms. Just like an avant-garde marine vessel equipped with state-of-the-art nautical instruments, you have been hard-wired with resiliency characteristics deep within your spirit that enable you to persevere through degrees of adversity you never imagined you'd be able to withstand. And the only way to truly find out what you are equipped to handle is to go through it. Weights are used to measure muscle strength and resistance is used to determine power. You won't know what's in you until you are battle tested. God will decide which giants you face, you will have to decide how you are going to face those giants: in fear and resentment, or with great resolve and unreserved resiliency.

Either way, standing between you and your dance with destiny are giants of no ordinary stature.

13-Foot Coffins

Buried in the Old Testament is an obscure passage that I doubt made it on your Scriptural memorization plan this past year. It probably wasn't in your Sunday School class curriculum, and if it was, your teacher may have scurried over it. It has utterly no implications on major biblical doctrines, and yet this passage fascinates me:

> Then we turned and went up the way to Bashan. And Og the king of Bashan came out against us, he and all his people, to battle at Edrei. But the Lord said to me, 'Do not fear him, for I have given him and all his people and his land into your hand. And you shall do to him as you did to Sihon the king of the Amorites, who lived at Heshbon.' So the Lord our God gave into our hand Og also, the king of Bashan, and all his people, and we struck him down until he had no survivor left. And we took all his cities at that time—there was not a city that we did not take from them—sixty cities, the whole region of Argob, the kingdom of Og in Bashan. All these were cities fortified with high walls, gates, and bars, besides very many unwalled villages. And we devoted them to destruction, as we did to Sihon the king of Heshbon, devoting to destruction every city, men, women, and children. But all the livestock and the spoil of the cities we took as our plunder. So we took the land at that time out of the hand of the two kings of the Amorites who were beyond the Jordan, from the Valley of the Arnon to Mount Hermon (the Sidonians call Hermon Sirion, while the Amorites call it Senir), all the cities of the tableland and all Gilead and all Bashan, as far as Salecah and Edrei, cities of the kingdom of Og in Bashan. (For only Og the king of Bashan was left of the remnant of the Rephaim. Behold, his bed was a bed of iron. Is it not in Rabbah of the Ammonites? Nine cubits was its

length, and four cubits its breadth, according to the common cubit. (Deuteronomy 3:1-11 ESV)

Notice that all the cities the Israelites were to take had "high walls, gates, and bars." This was no ministry picnic! It wouldn't be a Sunday walk in the park. Standing between the Israelites and their God-given destiny were towering walls and gargantuan nemeses; "Giants" in laymen terms!

Giants were common in the Old Testament. The Bible describes that as the Israelites in their Exodus came to the country east of the Jordan, near Heshbon, King Sihon of the Amorites refused to let them pass through his country. The Israelites fought him in a battle, gaining complete victory. His walled towns were captured and the complete Amorite country was taken by the Israelites, underscoring that the possession of the Promised Land has begun. The conquests of Sihon and Og give the Israelites a model of the future conquest under Joshua. Unlike its experience 38 years previously at Kadesh, Israel is not to fear the enemy. If God fights, victory is assured!

The term Amorites is used in the Bible to refer to certain highland mountaineers who inhabited the land of Canaan, described in Genesis 10:16 as descendants of Canaan, son of Ham. They are described as a powerful people of great stature "like the height of the cedars," who had occupied the land east and west of the Jordan. And now their king, Og, being described as the last "of the remnant of the giants," is slain by the Israelites.

The land of Bashan was famous for its prized cattle and oak groves. Lions also once roamed the area in ancient times. Og's kingdom was now given to the tribes of Reuben, Gad and the half-tribe of Manasseh (Num. 21:32-35; Deut. 3:1-13). Og's destruction is chanted in ballads of praise and song (Ps. 135:11; 136:20) as one of many great victories for the nation of Israel. In the book of Amos, chapter 2, verse 9, there seems to be a symbolic reference to Og as "The Amorite" whose height was like the height of the cedars and whose strength was like the oaks.

We read from this passage that Og's bed of iron was over thirteen feet (4m) long and six feet (1.8m) wide. Some scholars believe this refers to his coffin while others are sold on the literal translation that it refers to his bed. At any rate, we can safely conclude that if this giant needed a 13-foot bed to sleep in, he would also need a 13-foot coffin to be buried in.

Pause and reflect on the following statement for a moment and let its truth sink deeply into your spirit, swelling a quiet and confident resolve:

Every giant you will ever face in your lifetime, God has already picked out a coffin for its final burial. And the bigger the giant, the bigger the coffin. The bigger the coffin, the more glory God gets!

The giants in your life serve a purpose.

What God Is After

Before we can have the courage to face the giants in our lives we must know what we are made for and what God is after. Only then will we find the courage to face every "Og" in our lives. Remember; the smaller the giant, the less glory God gets. The bigger the giant, the more glory God gets in our lives. He is after much glory.

When God hardened Pharaoh's heart to keep him from cooperating with Moses, God wasn't just trying to make it hard on Moses for the sake of frustration; God was setting the stage for himself to receive greater glory in the end. When God made the Israelites face giants before gaining possession of the Promised

Land, it wasn't because God wanted the Israelites to cower in their own fear but rather he wanted them to confide in His sovereign muscles that He wanted to flex for them. He wanted them to learn to trust him to the point that their faith triumphed over their fears.

Think about this for a moment: if David didn't muster up the faith and courage to face Goliath, some other shepherd boy would've gotten the job done. If Esther weren't willing to step into her divine purpose "for such a time as this," God would've raised up another queen who would have had the boldness to stand before the King of Persia and fight for the honor of the Jews in such a critical time in history. If Moses didn't go, God would've found someone who would. If Peter wouldn't become the "Rock" that Jesus would plant his church upon, then God would've called someone else. If Martin Luther refused to confront indulgence salesman Johann Tetzel with his Ninety-Five Theses in 1517 and become the catalyst for the Reformation, we'd be reading about someone else in church history who did. The reason being is this: God isn't going to be robbed of His glory. And your playing small to your giants doesn't bring glory and honor to God.

He will get his glory. We have the privilege of facing our giants with faith, or cowering in fear while God raises up somebody else to do the job. God is not limited by time, we are. He controls the timeline. That's why when the first generation of Israelites who came out of Egypt were too scared to go into Canaan because of the stature of the giants, God let them die off and waited patiently forty years until a younger generation would come along who had the guts to face the giants. You and I may not have forty years, but God does. He has all the time He chooses. And He isn't going to be robbed of his glory. When He calls us to be a part of His timeline, we get to stand up and face our giants, or run in fear. Nonetheless, He will find someone brave enough to stand up against the "Ogs" in every generation whether we choose to or not.

That's the purpose of the giants in your life. You can face them with courage and let God get his glory, or you can step aside and let another take your place. My prayer is that this book helps you to muster up the courage and faith to face the giants God has meant for you to slay. Will you step into God's timeline and face your giants with reckless abandon?

His glory is at stake!

Chapter Two
Abandonment and Fatherlessness

Life is not a matter of holding good cards, but of playing a poor hand well.
~ Robert Louis Stevenson

We are not animals. We are not a product of what has happened to us in our past. We have the power of choice. ~ Stephen Covey

I was born to a teenage mother on Christmas day in 1970. I had a sister who was ten months older than me. When I was six-months-old my biological father left us, leaving my seventeen-year-old mother the strenuous burden of caring for two toddlers all by herself. Needless to say, she had to drop out of high school and go to work to provide for her young family. Still being a "child" herself, Mom had incredible giants in front of her. Giants that she would be willing to rise up and face boldly one by one, day by day, and week by week.

Growing up in Baltimore, Maryland I was a lover of hard shell blue crabs, summer visits to Ocean City, and baseball. And as James Earl Jones introspectively ruminated in the film *Field of Dreams*, baseball was "the one constant through all the years."

On an average, we moved about once every two years. But no matter where we lived I always found a place to play baseball. I had childhood dreams of playing for the Orioles one day at the old Memorial Stadium on 33rd Street. Baseball was my passion. It was my life. Going to ballgames was like going to Disney World for me. The ballpark was my fantasyland away from home. It was my "Field of Dreams." When I was there, the world seemed to me a place of pointed destiny rather than a metropolis of random coincidence. It was here amidst the peanuts, cracker jacks, and cotton candy that I learned to dream... to believe... to imagine.

It's been said that dreams are the language of the Holy Spirit. Every model and make of human beings comes with a built-in hardwiring of imagination. It's where we learn to dream. I believe it's the standardized equipment necessary to successfully navigate through all of life's hardships. Dreams are where we find hope, inspiration, fortitude, and the resolve to live a life of purpose and meaning. It's no wonder the enemy spends so much time attacking our dreams; they are the Holy Spirit's language of creativity and imagination, conveying in our hearts a picture of something extraordinary that the Creator of the universe invites us to be a part of. Henry David Thoreau understood this when he observed, "It is usually the imagination that is wounded first, rather than the heart; it being much more sensitive."

It's in our imagination, the maternity ward of our dreams, that we will fight some of life's grandest battles. If the enemy can win there he can keep us from ever attempting anything epic for God, thus reducing us to mere survivalist creatures, shrinking our journey here on earth to nothing more than coping mechanisms and weathering techniques. And while we all need to grow in the area of coping skills, life was meant to be so much more than just coping, or merely getting by.

My dreams were cultivated on a little league field. After every practice I stood in line at the concession stand to buy *Topps* baseball cards with the bubble gum inside. I didn't care too much about the gum, I just loved to collect cards of pro baseball players and imagine being in their shoes one day, traveling from city to city, playing in the "bigs," staring down Nolan Ryan, calling my shot like Babe Ruth, and pelting grand slams into the bleachers of packed out stadiums. When I dreamed, I dreamed big and with great intensity. This deeply agitated my fifth grade teacher, especially when she had to awaken me from a temporary retreat to fantasyland during class as my snoring disrupted a math lesson she was trying to facilitate.

I would spend countless hours in the backyard emulating the batting styles of Oriole greats' Eddie Murray, Ken Singleton, and Cal Ripken, Jr. Then I would try to make good on those imitations on the diamond at North Glen, the little league complex up the road from where we lived. When I wasn't playing baseball, I was organizing my baseball cards I bought from the concession at North Glen.

Little league was not only the place where I lived out my most sacred childhood dreams, it was also responsible for my first conscious awareness of abandonment: being fatherless.

Growing up without a dad didn't mean much to me at first because I didn't know any better. How can you miss what you don't know you're assumed to have? I didn't know kids were supposed to have fathers because I never had one around. Its kind of hard to miss what you never knew existed in the first place. It wasn't until little league ball that I began to sense awareness of a deep void and internal wound in my life. It was seeing the other boys on my team having a relationship with their dads and seeing those dads cheer their sons on at our baseball games that made me attuned to that void in my life.

This is where the first 13-foot giant I would face reared its ugly head in my childhood. This conscious awareness birthed a sense of abandonment in my life. I hadn't seen the movie *Good Will Hunting* and I didn't know *it wasn't my fault.* I was now conscious of the fact that I was different from the other kids.

I lacked something.

Something was abnormal about me.

I didn't belong.

I didn't fit in.

These thoughts perplexed me. And I believed it *was* somehow my fault. These thoughts became internalized bullets; assaulting the very purity of my imagination while diminishing my ability to focus everywhere from the playground to the classroom. Over time, my grades went down, my attitude shifted, and my self-esteem plummeted. In essence, I adopted a "quitters" mentality that affected me for years. If things got difficult, I simply quit. I eventually even gave up on baseball, the one dream that was a place of tranquility and solace for me.

Abandonment is a dream killer and an identity assassin; a giant that millions of young people in our generation have fallen victim to. It stabs at the core of our being and tells us we are valueless creatures. I'm not sure if anything on earth devalues us more than the feeling of being abandoned. If only we were "good enough" people, others wouldn't have abandoned us. If we had "value" they wouldn't have deserted us. Yet we are left alone to ponder how unworthy we are. Left to these deceptive deductions and ungodly lies from hell, we shrink into a defensive and guarded posture of living, protecting any ounce of self worth that may be lingering. If we are to live offensively and take up our dance with destiny we must learn to overcome this "Og" in our lives.

In facing the giant of abandonment, we must recognize that those who have walked out on us do not determine our personal value; it is measured solely by the One Who created us and fatefully gave His life for us. And the course we choose based on our estimation of that value will have eternal dividends.

Monkey Business

In his book *Put Your Dream to the Test*, author John Maxwell wrote about an experiment conducted with a group of monkeys. Four monkeys were placed in a room that had a tall pole in the center. Suspended from the top of that pole was a bunch of bananas.

One of the hungry monkeys started climbing the pole to get something to eat, but just as he reached out to grab a banana, he was doused with a torrent of cold water. Squealing, he scampered down the pole and abandoned his attempt to feed himself. Each monkey made a similar attempt, and each one was drenched with cold water. After making several attempts, they finally gave up.

Then researchers removed one of the monkeys from the room and replaced him with a new monkey. As the newcomer began to climb the pole, the other three grabbed him and pulled him down to the ground. After trying to climb the pole several times and being dragged down by the others, he finally gave up and never attempted to climb the pole again.

The researchers replaced the original monkeys, one by one, with new ones, and each time a new monkey was brought in, the others would drag him down before he could reach the bananas. In time, only monkeys who had never received a cold shower were in the room, but none of them would climb the pole. They prevented one another from climbing, but none of them knew why.[i]

Perhaps *dream killers* have beaten you down. Maybe you don't even look up at the banana anymore. It's too painful to see it in your mind only to never be able to climb the pole. Maybe you've convinced yourself the bananas aren't real, you ration that dreams are for kids and once we get to a certain age we're not supposed to dream anymore. I believe this kind of morbid capitulation echoes

Albert Schweitzer's inference, "The tragedy of life is what dies inside a man while he lives."

Albert Einstein concluded, "Logic will get you from A to B. Imagination will take you everywhere." Mark Twain would seem to agree, "You can't depend on your eyes when your imagination is out of focus."

Your imagination matters…

Your ability to dream and imagine is not only vital to your survival on this earth, but also essential to your becoming fully alive; the resilient warrior God is shaping you to become. In our era, it's not easy to find time to dream. Our imaginations are constantly under siege, whether it be hectic work schedules, multitasking overload, or just simply not enough margin in our lives. Or as is the case with issues of abandonment, we don't even feel worthy to dream. Nonetheless, we were made to dream, and our dance with destiny is contingent upon us keeping our imagination alive. From it springs forth our dreams, hopes, and eternal legacy.

A Good Kick in The Teeth

You were made for something so much greater than just surviving. You were made to thrive. Not without adversity, and not just despite it… yet because of it. You don't have to view adversity as a threat. It's not some hurdle you need to find your way around. It's a strategic and necessary vault in your life that can catapult you into higher levels of living if you allow it. This requires a healthy view of adversity and a maturing response to it.

My daughter is a gymnast (she won the all-around 2010 Level 5 state championship meet in Nashville, I'm proud to say). Gymnasts must be retrained in the area of instincts. Our bodies inherently tend to shun running full speed into things physically… that's a good thing unless you have some kind of bizarre fetish with plowing into brick walls. Our instincts tell us to slow down when approaching an unmovable obstacle. That's why gymnasts have to be retrained to go full speed ahead, thrusting all their inward force and physical strength into the vault so that they can get the best possible lift off the vault. The higher the lift, the better the score. But you don't get maximum lift without fully thrusting yourself into the vault.

I believe we need to be retrained in how we view adversity. If we see it as a hurdle, we do whatever we must to get around it, or run from it. It doesn't do anything for us. It doesn't shape us, change us, or catapult us into something extraordinary. But when we view adversity as a vault and channel our spiritual and psychological energies toward engaging adversity positively, we thrust ourselves into each trial with the right attitude, expecting it to catapult us to higher levels of living, greater accomplishments, and most importantly, more conformity to the likeness of Christ.

> Count it all joy, my brothers, when you meet trials of various kinds, for you know that the testing of your faith produces steadfastness. And let steadfastness have its full effect, that you may be perfect and complete, lacking in nothing. (James 1:2-4 ESV)

God's purpose in trials is that we mature and lack nothing.

Walt Disney, the most decorated dreamer in modern history, found that his greatest ideas were birthed out of his greatest struggles. He once hailed, "All the adversity I've had in my life, all my troubles and obstacles, have strengthened me… You may not realize it when it happens, but a kick in the teeth may be the best thing in the world for you."

Walt drove the company by embracing risk, and his brother, Roy, lost his hair by trying to balance Walt's enthusiasm. It seemed to everyone, including Roy, that just when things were going smoothly, Walt would find a way to court disaster yet again. Adversity became a way of life for Disney Studios. If he wasn't struggling, Walt wasn't happy.

In 1937, following the huge success of *Snow White*, overwhelming employee expectations were created that left Walt feeling powerless to fulfill. In 1941 Disney Studio animators went on strike. Walt was shattered. He would never again feel the same passion for cartoons and movies. Thus began his wilderness period, which lasted a decade. Out of that period came Walt's inspiration for *Disneyland*, and he threw himself relentlessly into the theme park idea.

For Walt, his greatest adversity always brought about his greatest ideas. Opposition for him always pushed him to greater levels of imagination and resolve. Perhaps that's why he was able to say with such grace, "I have been up against tough competition all my life. I wouldn't know how to get along without it."

What opposition or adversity are you facing today; perhaps your greatest idea and greatest inspiration will come out of this chapter in your life.

My son is taking Taekwondo so when the new *Karate Kid* movie came out we had to see it. In China, where the movie was filmed, it is better known by the title: *The Kung Fu Dream*. The plot centers around a twelve-year-old boy named Dre, from Detroit, who moves to China with his mother and runs afoul with a group of bullies. The character, played by Jaden Smith, gets the tar beat out of him on the playground. Embarrassed and humiliated, everything in him wants to run and hide from his tormenter. He hates living in this unfamiliar place, and he cries out for his mother to take him back to America.

As the saga unfolds, he finds an unlikely ally in an aging maintenance man named Mr. Han, played by Jackie Chan, a kung fu master who teaches him the secrets of self-defense. Then we begin to see a gradual transition in the film where Dre evolves from simply wanting to defend himself into being a part of something much more glorious and far more epic than he ever imagined. He will ultimately get to dance with destiny as he is afforded the opportunity to face his nemesis in a kung fu tournament.

Dre finds himself taking hard knocks all along this epic journey, culminating in a championship bout with his rival. In the match, he is wounded and carried back to the dressing room. The doctor advises that he should not go back into the tournament, which would by default crown his rival as the champion. But Dre wants to return to the match.

That's when Mr. Han affirms him: "You've already accomplished everything you wanted to. Why do you still want to fight?"

Dre responds: "Because win or lose, I don't want to be afraid any more. And I'm still afraid."

Every time Dre gets back up after being knocked down he finds himself fearing less, and braving more. So it is with you and me. God is more concerned with preparing you for your life's dance with destiny than insulating you from pain and discomfort. He wants us to become resilient people who fear less and brave more. Therefore life cannot be reduced to merely "not getting beat up," which most of our defense mechanisms are built around. There's more at stake... there's a greater glory... a bigger picture... and a BIGGER God we serve.

We all get beat up. We all fail. We all fall down. But it's resilient people who are changing the world. It's not the people walking through life unscathed who are shaping eternity. The people untouched by adversity aren't shaping eternity; it's being shaped by dogged resilient people, who, under constant fire from the enemy, just keep coming. They refuse to quit! That's the kind of person God is in the business of shaping: resilient warriors.

God's Sovereignty in HD

I don't know if there is a character in the Old Testament who may have had more abandonment issues than Joseph. The youngest of twelve brothers, Joseph was ridiculously spoiled by his father, Jacob. He was given a robe of many colors to signify his father's favoritism, a gesture that didn't help Joseph out in regards to sibling rivalry. His brothers despised him because he was Daddy's favorite.

When Joseph was seventeen-years-old, God conceived a dream in his heart, and even though Joseph didn't understand all the ramifications of his dream at the time, he was convinced that his life had a divine purpose to it… a dance with destiny. When he shared his dream with the rest of the family his brothers hated him all the more, especially the part about them one day bowing down to Joseph!

One day they conspired a plot to kill Joseph. They would kill him, dip his robe in animal blood, and tell their father an animal mauled him to death. When Joseph came out to the fields they were pasturing, his brothers beat him to a bloody pulp and threw him into a pit. They would've finished him off if the older sibling, Rueben, hadn't intervened. Spotting a caravan of Ishmaelites coming up the road, Rueben talked his brothers into selling Joseph to them. Consequently, Joseph is taken to Egypt and sold into slavery.

But God is *with* Joseph – the most significant piece of the story.

He becomes prosperous in all of his work prompting his master, Potiphar, to appoint him head over Potiphar's entire household. And just when it feels like Joseph is getting his life back on track, making something for himself and succeeding in his business, Potiphar's wife falsely accuses Joseph of making sexual advances on her. Joseph is thrown into prison where he will spend the next couple of years.

If he hadn't given up on his dream after his brothers nearly killed him, being falsely accused and imprisoned should knock him down for the ten count, right? No, Joseph continues to fuel his life with inspiration. He believes His God is with him despite every attack. Joseph understands that in this lifetime you will often be attacked because you are doing the right things, not just because something is wrong.

Most of our modern theology has taught us that when things are going wrong we must not be doing something right. We aren't playing our spiritual cards right. We aren't memorizing enough Scripture. We aren't praying hard enough. We don't have enough faith. While we need to meditate on God's word (Joshua 1:8), pray with impudence (Luke 11:8), and grow our faith, it is a grave misnomer to think that because we are doing these things that they will somehow insulate us from pain, hardship, and adversity. Remember, we were made to face giants, not hide from them in our caves of religious fidelity.

Joseph kept believing, kept trusting, and kept hoping. Joseph let his hopes, not his hurts, shape his future. In prison, Joseph wasn't surrounded by society's most gifted motivational speakers or encouraging orators. He didn't get daily Tweets on how to remain positive amidst such piercing pain. He wasn't subscribing to any motivational blogs. Hope wasn't exactly bouncing off the walls in a prison cell. There's always a scarcity of hope in the dungeon.

That's why it takes intentionality to find inspiration in the pits and prisons of life. Inspiration is fuel that you must dig down deep for in the mire of life. It's doesn't come easy. But it's essential to becoming a resilient person in life.

In September of 1942, a young doctor, his new wife, his mother, father, and brother, were arrested in Vienna and taken to a Nazi concentration camp. The man was Viktor Emil Frankl, who would later write one of the most influential books of our time: *Man's Search for Meaning*.

Throughout his experience in the death camps, Frankl could not help but see, that, among those given a chance for survival, it was those who held on to a vision of the future; whether it be a significant task before them, or a return to their loved ones; that were most likely to survive their suffering. Frankl lost his wife, his parents, and other members of his family to the Holocaust, and it was the meaning he found in that suffering that led to the writing of *Man's Search for Meaning*.

I believe Joseph was holding on to a vision of the future while in prison. I think he was still holding on to his dream. It had taken some blows. He had been emotionally scarred. Nothing seemed to be in his favor at the moment. But Joseph held on to the dream. He didn't quit!

Joseph's time was coming.

Eventually, Joseph encounters a couple of Pharaoh's servants in prison. One morning at chow time, both Pharaoh's cupbearer and chief baker are troubled over the dreams they had the night before. "We have had dreams, and there is no one to interpret them," they agonize as Joseph takes a bite out of his moldy toast and stale jelly. Joseph replies, "Do not interpretations belong to God? Please tell them to me."

Long story short, Joseph interprets their dreams exactly the way they are to unfold and the prophecies come to pass with pinpoint precision. Some time later, Pharaoh has a troubling dream and when there is no one in the land to interpret, Pharaoh's cupbearer remembers Joseph. He is brought before the king and not only rightly interprets the dream; he is appointed second in command over all of Egypt.

God revealed to Joseph there would be seven years of abundance followed by seven years of famine. Under Joseph's leadership, the Egyptians would store up much grain in preparation for the famine, and then when the famine came, people from all over the world would come to Egypt in search for food, and Joseph would be in charge of its distribution.

This famine brought Joseph's family to Egypt. He is reunited with his family and their lives are spared. Soon after Jacob dies, Joseph's brothers fear that Joseph will exact vengeance upon them in retribution for their wicked actions against him way back in Dothan.

> When Joseph's brothers saw that their father was dead, they said, "It may be that Joseph will hate us and pay us back for all the evil that we did to him." So they sent a message to Joseph, saying, "Your father gave this command before he died, 'Say to Joseph, Please forgive the transgression of your brothers and their sin, because they did evil to you.' And now, please forgive the transgression of the servants of the God of your father." Joseph wept when they spoke to him. His brothers also came and fell down before him and said, "Behold, we are your servants." But Joseph said to them, "Do not fear, for am I in the place of God? As for you, you meant evil against me, but God meant it for good, to bring it about that many people should be kept alive, as they are today. So do not fear; I will provide for you and your little ones." Thus he comforted them and spoke kindly to them. (Genesis 50:15-21 ESV)

Resilient people have a "Big Picture" view of life, and because Joseph had a *High-Definition* angle on the sovereignty of God, he understood that God uses even the ill-conceived intentions of others to paint the redemptive canvas of our lives.

One of the greatest lessons we can learn from Joseph's life is that there will always be more opportunities to quit than there are opportunities to conquer. Our dreams are always filled with detours and surprises, setbacks and hardships. But we can be assured that if our dream comes from God, the dream holds us when we feel unable to hold it.

In his book *Running With The Giants*[ii], John Maxwell notes that Joseph could trust the heart of God even when he couldn't trace the hand of God. Consider his journey and its detours:

> Misunderstood by his family
> > Give up?
> Sold into slavery by his brothers
> > Give up?
> Living in a strange country far from home – Give up?
> Given favor in Potiphar's house – Go on!
> Wrongly accused by Potiphar's wife – Give up?
> Thrown into prison – Give up?
> Put in charge of all the prisoners – Go on!
> Forgotten by the chief butler – Give up?
> Remained in prison two years – Give up?
> Interpreted Pharaoh's dream – Go on!
> Became second in command of Egypt – Go on!

Why didn't Joseph give up? What kept him going? After all, like many of us, he had twice as many *give-ups* as *go-ons*. Every God-inspired dream will have its share of negative surprises and discouraging detours. I believe the key is this: even though Joseph found himself in twice as many "give-up" moments than "go-on" moments, scripture says "the Lord was with Joseph" and Joseph trusted God even when it didn't make any sense to him. He planted himself in God's growth process and developed himself during the down times. He knew that God's timetable was different from his, but that didn't take away the human side of feeling discouraged or disheartened. And yet that's why the Bible calls it endurance:

> Therefore, since we are surrounded by so great a cloud of witnesses, let us also lay aside every weight, and sin which clings so closely, and let us run with endurance the race that is set before us, looking to Jesus, the founder and perfecter of our faith, who for the joy that was set before him endured the cross, despising the shame, and is seated at the right hand of the throne of God. Consider him who endured from sinners such hostility against himself, so that you may not grow weary or fainthearted. (Hebrews 12:1-3 ESV)

Joseph endured despite the human side of feeling fatigued, discouraged, and abandoned. He held on and his dream ultimately saved many people (Genesis 50:20). History was shaped by his faithfulness. And the realization of his dream was sweeter than anything he had ever visualized or imagined. Martin Luther King, Jr. once hailed, "If you lose hope, somehow you lose the vitality that keeps life moving, you lose that courage to be, that quality that helps you go on in spite of it all. And so today I still have a dream."

Joseph faced harsh abandonment, false accusations, and unjust imprisonment. Nonetheless, he could forgive. He could heal. He could love. He overcome the odds against him and faced the giant of abandonment because of his view on the sovereignty of God. So can you!

And we know that for those who love God all things work together for good, for those who are called according to his purpose. For those whom he foreknew he also predestined to be conformed to the image of his Son, in order that he might be the firstborn among many brothers. And those whom he predestined he also called, and those whom he called he also justified, and those whom he justified he also glorified. (Romans 8:28-30 ESV)

Your time is coming; guard your imagination and hold on to your God-inspired dreams! After all, dreams are the language of the Holy Spirit.

Before I could learn to dream again, I had to overcome a giant much bigger than an absentee father; I would have to learn to stand toe to toe with a physically and verbally abusive tyrant, and this bully was a much more savage Goliath than any other giant I would ever face in my entire life.

Chapter Three
It's a Cruel World After All

You may trod me in the very dirt... But still, like dust, I'll rise. ~ Maya Angelou

It is our willing permission, our consent to what happens to us, that hurts us far more than what happens to us in the first place. ~ Victor Frankl

Any form of abuse is an awful injustice in our broken world.

Whether it is the bully in the schoolyard, a battered wife, a young girl who has been sexually assaulted, helpless victims of sex trafficking, or the powerless child suffering violent blows from a parent in a fit of rage. It's never pretty.

In my case, it was the latter.

Now I'm not the type of person who believes that any form of physical punishment is abusive. I got paddled several times in elementary school and it by no means was misconstrued as abuse to me. I perceived it as correction and I took my punishment like a "man" just like any fourth grader would: I cried like a baby and then *partially* repented (a theological oxymoron) for flying paper airplanes in class and throwing spit balls at my teachers!

There's much dialogue today about when exactly physical punishment becomes physical abuse. I'm not an authority on the issue, but I do know this: any physical contact or verbal assaults from a parent that cause extreme emotional, mental, or psychological trauma, is beyond the scope of punishment, and assuredly abusive.

When I was twelve-years-old, my mother sat my sister and I down and gave us the news that she was going to remarry our biological father. His marriage with his second wife had dissolved and my mother felt it would be to our advantage to have him in our lives. What's more, he would be getting custody of the two children from his second marriage and we would all come together like the *Brady Bunch* and become one big family, living happily ever after behind a white picket fence in a Maryland suburb. What we didn't realize is that this was only the beginning of what would become several years of malicious custody battles with his ex-wife, domestic violence within our home, and vicious environments for any child to have to endure.

My mother's decision to give my father a second chance actually incited emotions I had never really had before. For the first time in my life, I would have my *real* father living with us. What would that look like? How would things change? Would my dad take me to baseball games? Would he let me play his drum set? Would we go camping together? Would our lives become more stable after having to relocate so many times?

At first, it seemed like it would be exhilarating having him around. I would have something in my life I never experienced before, a constant male figure. After all, having a father is something I dreamed of many times. But it didn't take long for me to realize this wasn't going to be a dream fulfilled, this was shaping up to be a nightmare on *Elm Street*.

We went from a fragmented family of three to a blended dysfunctional family of six in what seemed to be overnight.

Years later, after my parents divorced the second time, my mother would apologize to me for allowing him to come back into our lives. She didn't know him all that well during their six-month marriage as teenagers, but she had seen some abusive tendencies, having been struck by him with a barbeque rod and having him put a cigarette out in her face. But this was twelve years later, and to her credit, she believed that everyone deserved a chance to grow up and experience second chances. She believed that remarrying my dad would be the best thing for my sister and me.

After they remarried, my dad didn't seem very interested at all in becoming a father to us, but more eager to have my mother as a golden stepmother for the two children he fathered in his second marriage and now had custody over. This "Brady Bunch" wasn't going to mesh. The encyclopedia on family dysfunction was about to be written. And it would take years to be published.

Shortly after my parents remarried, I had my first encounter with my father's surreptitious wrath. All six of us, two adults and four children, were leaving my grandmother's house to go home after Thanksgiving dinner. I still wasn't all that comfortable around my dad, and since we had taken two vehicles, I told my mother I didn't want to ride with my dad, that I wanted to ride home with her. My father took that as some sort of personal rejection. He masked his irritation well, yet under his skin he was seething with anger. He took charge by demanding that I ride in the van with him and my half-brother, and the girls would ride with my mother. I had no idea what was about to happen.

My father stealthily took a separate route home than my mother. He took us down a quiet side street. When we got to an isolated rural area, he conveniently pulled the van over to the side of the road, put the transmission in park, came around to the side door of the van, yanked me out by my hair and threw me to the ground.

What came next was something that would scar me for years to come and begin a hardening like wax over my twelve-year old heart. I took a countless flurry of punches and kicks from this grown man right there on the side of the road. The few seconds it took for my father to steamroll me, from my inference, felt more like ten rounds with Mike Tyson in slow motion. Time seemed to stop. I lay balled up on the side of the road in shock and dismay. Looking back, I can't imagine how long this barrage of assaults would have continued if it weren't for a sympathetic passerby seeing this violent outburst and pulling over to intervene. I thought my father was going to punch him out, and he may have been thinking about it, but in nervous reluctance he grabbed me by the hair again, pulled me up out of the dirt and threw me back in the van, slamming the doors behind. He got back in the driver seat and we went home.

I was forewarned that if I mentioned any thing that happened that day to anyone, then I would suffer "further consequences." That's the nature of abuse; it reduces you to nothing more than an object that your villain can use, and misuse, and then forces you to keep silent with threats of intimidation.

After we got home, I was too terrified to share with my mother what had happened in fear of getting beat up again.

Over the next six months the beatings continued, gradually becoming more brutal, yet my father was always astute with his anger and clandestine about his rage. At first, he would vent his frustrations on me when nobody else was home, but when he could no longer hold out for that convenience, he started forcing me behind closed doors where others couldn't see. Nonetheless, they could still hear the bedlam. My mother was partly attuned to his uncontrollable temper and fits of rage, but she seemed to believe that things could grow into a state of relative normalcy if she remained calm and non-confrontal with my father. He was a masterful tactician at concealing his tracks, especially when the police showed up at our house one day after suspicious neighbors saw bruises on my arms and reported it. He was a skilled politician – a diplomat coming across as a very responsible and concerned parent of a "wild, rambunctious, and rebellious child," he would convince them. This was the picture he painted. He told the authorities my bruises were from playing neighborhood football with the kids, and because he was a convincing politician in addition to the fact that we lived in a middle class neighborhood, the police bought it. To them, my father appeared to be a decent law-abiding citizen just trying to manage typical adolescent rebellion in Suburbia, USA. They couldn't see what went on behind closed doors. This pattern instilled within me a feeling of being trapped in a cage. One that seemed hopeless to ever break out of.

It didn't take long for me to become distrustful of adults or authority figures in general. Especially my father, who managed to masquerade his viciousness, or the police officers that were so easily hoodwinked. They didn't believe my testimony over the slick-talking treatises my father offered them whenever they were called out to our house for domestic incidents. And I would always get beat worse after they left, this being my father's method of bullying me and intimidating me not to cry out again. Getting away with this form of abuse emboldened my father's physical tirades as well as his psychological mastery over my mind. I was constantly being dehumanized with his verbal assaults:

"You're just a sissy."

"You little fag."

"You're a *ussy."

"You worthless piece of @*#&!"

These constant verbal slurs were like arrows in my heart, an attempt on his part to break me down to nothing more than a crippled animal, something less than human. What's more, he seemed to get some kind of sick gratification out of maiming my spirit with these taunts.

As I turned thirteen-years-old, I adopted the conviction that nobody was out for me. Nobody could be trusted. If I were going to escape this horror, I would have to make my own way out.

The Crazy Train

Amidst all this tension in our home, my sister had issues of her own. She became bulimic, leading my father to put a literal lock and chain on the refrigerator. Bulk amounts of food were frequently missing; especially the sweets, and we would have "family meetings" to get to the bottom of everything. These meetings weren't actual family discussion, just intense lecturing channels for my father to vent.

One evening before my mother got home, I saw my father coming out of the bedroom with an empty cartoon of ice cream he had just finished off. I wouldn't have thought anything of it if he hadn't appeared to be trying to hide it behind his back. It raised my suspicion as to whether my sister was getting blamed for some of his private binging. Later that night, an issue about food disappearing came up again and I ratted out my father for eating all the ice cream. I wasn't going to let my sister take the blame for this one! My dad exploded across the room in an agitated fury, slugged the back of my head, grabbed me by the arm and dragged me downstairs into the utility room. Once in the privacy of that room, he pounded on me ruthlessly. I quickly dropped to the floor from the blows, but then he kicked me several times before finally letting up. I was scared to move, fearing more retribution for my crime. He rapidly fired off some profanities, called me a few emasculating names, then marched back upstairs. I lay there for the next forty-five minutes in a state of dread.

I knew I must do something. His outbursts were getting more violent and the dehumanizing of my spirit was settling in. I decided to take matters into my own hands.

I would run away.

I was thirteen when I ran away from home for the first time. It was about thirty miles to my grandmother's apartment. The next morning my mother picked me up and informed me that my father had arranged (he had paid a psychologist to admit me) for me to spend the next few months in a counseling facility in Washington, D.C. My mother informed me is was more like a *country club*. I found out soon after it was a psychiatric institute for children. This inflamed my anger toward my father.

"The crazy man was making me look like the crazy one," I mused. Have you ever seen the movie *What About Bob*? If you have, then you get the picture!

Like many teens in crisis, I used music to escape my reality. Ozzy Osbourne's lyrics draped my mind:

> *Mental wounds still screaming*
> *Driving me insane;*
> *I'm going off the rails on a crazy train*
> *I'm going off the rails on a crazy train*

I was going off the rails all right.

I had typical issues with adolescent rebellion (of which I later learned to take responsibility for), but my rebellion was perpetually intensified by my father's violence and his illusory cover up tactics.

I did what I had to do at P.I.W. (Psychiatric Institute of Washington). I even took the medication they put me on… whatever that was. I also had some fun. Anytime someone new was entering the building, we all acted like animals, foaming at the mouth and bouncing off windowsills. We put on a great show. One time a girl who was being admitted by her mother saw our lunacy and ran right back out the front door, yelling "No way, Mama, I ain't goin' in there!"

Shamefully, it was some of the best fun I had as a thirteen-year-old. While other eighth graders were going on field trips, I was trippin' myself at the psychiatric ward. Sometimes I look back now and actually miss all that fun… kind of scary, huh?

Three months later, I came home and was hounded daily about whether I had taken my meds or not. If only they could have invented a pill that made my father disappear. I would've swallowed the whole bottle, chewed up the capsules like popcorn, and chased it with a bottle of peppermint schnapps.

These were truly some of the most traumatic days of my life, but I have learned a great secret over the years, that if you can't find some element of humor in your pain, you can't fully heal. Laughter is like *good* medicine, the Bible tells us (Proverbs 17:22).

The only thing I learned at P.I.W. is that all the treatment it afforded would never make my father stop beating me. The only way to escape that was to keep running away. So I got bolder, ran farther, and ran more often.

The Sunshine State

Just before my sophomore year in high school, we packed up the U-Haul and moved to Florida. It did feel somewhat like a new beginning for our family. But like any new chapter in your life, if you don't change the way you do things, you end up with the same results. "Insanity is doing the same thing, over and over again, but expecting different results," Albert Einstein noted. A change of scenery, geography, or physical surroundings doesn't change people or human hearts. It only changes the landscape of your problems and gives you a different backdrop. For me, that meant running away to Grandma's house was no longer a thirty-mile journey but a 1,000-mile escapade.

I would definitely need a bigger suitcase!

I tried out and made the JV football squad. I loved playing football and it kept me away from home more. That helped me avoid turbulent confrontations with my father... for a little while anyway. Our team went 1-9 that year. I don't recollect all the details but I think our one win was against a team whose bus broke down and had to forfeit... or something like that.

Not a lot of motivational stories came out of my football career at Springstead High School. Our team was pathetic. We were so bad the only thing our coach could talk about at pep rallies was how pretty our cheerleaders were. Which, in itself, was a little weird and... somewhat creepy. But maybe it was our fault for not giving our coach much to talk about when it came to football. I think our team had more unsportsmanlike conduct penalties called against each other in one game than we had on opposing teams all season long. Talk about imploding! We were ugly, but it beat hanging out at home where I would be an easy target for my father's rage whenever he imploded. He was a ticking time bomb and I didn't want to be around when it went off.

Unfortunately, I couldn't avoid his presence all the time.

One day he really lost it and beat me to a pulp. I was wearing nothing but a pair of shorts and it was raining torrentially outside. I took all that I could and made a beeline for the side door of the garage (my father preferred to do his physical work on me in the garage where it was less obvious to the rest of the family). I took off out into the rain not knowing where to go from there. But I knew I had to find a way back to Maryland where I had family from my mother's side who could take me in.

I went out to the nearest highway and started hitchhiking north. A by-passer picked me up and asked where I was heading.

"I need to get to Maryland," I tried to say in my best independent, adult-like voice.

Noticing I was barefoot, shirtless, shoeless, and very *green* at hitchhiking (I had been hitchhiking from the median in the middle of the road), it didn't take a nuclear engineer to figure out I was a runaway; not to mention I was fourteen-years-old. The fellow successfully talked me into turning myself in at the police station and convinced me that they would protect me from my father. Feeling somewhat safe in his presence, I obliged.

The authorities would have to do some investigating on my case so I was temporarily placed in a shelter home where I managed to get some clothes. After a couple of days I was informed that the authorities were going to send me back home and that I just had to "deal with it."

I wasn't up for "dealing" with my father anymore. I launched out of the transport car that was supposed to take me home and ran into the nearby woods. Fortunately for me, the escort was overweight and very out of shape. I could outrun him. I was "free" again to resume my trek to Maryland where I would find my "independence" and liberty, and have all of my problems vanish as I chewed on Grandma's chocolate chip cookies.

Grandma was an amazing woman.

She seemed to believe in me when it felt like nobody else did. Even when I was at my worst, Grandma always treated me like I was special. Like I was valued. Like my life had purpose to it. She loved me unconditionally when I didn't even know what that word meant. She was a woman of indescribable quiet strength and an almost mystical spiritual fortitude. And I know that it was Grandma's prayers that kept me alive as a fourteen-year-old runaway roaming the streets of Atlanta, Nashville, Washington D.C., and Baltimore.

I had no idea the danger I had made myself susceptible to as a teenage runaway. I was scared, but my desperation and quest for "freedom" seemed to trump my consciousness of fear. Fueled by sheer adrenaline, I hitchhiked from one city to the next. I was even picked up by a pedophile one time that made advances at me and tried to put his hands on my thigh. I was out of that car "quicker than a fat kid in a game of dodge ball," as a student in my youth group used to say. I bailed out and the weirdo drove off hastily. I felt fortunate to be alive. I had read stories about things that happened to teenage runaways who weren't as fortunate as I to escape their predators. Looking back, I know it wasn't luck. I attribute my safety to Grandma's fervent prayers and God's grace.

It was at this time that I first began to see God's fingerprints in my life.

Bubba... More Than a Shrimp Market Guru!

We've all become familiar with *Forrest Gump's* "bigger than life" friendship with Bubba. Well, my story also has a *Bubba* in it… and it doesn't entail an overabundance of shrimp, but it does involve heaps of pizza and an enduring act of compassion.

Early one evening, as dusk painted a breathtaking scene of purple and orange strokes across the canvas of Nashville's skyline, this teenage runaway was about to see God's fingerprints in something beyond a picturesque sunset… I would see His fingerprints in a person… a very unusual person. It all started when I was offered a lift from a burly truck driver heading east on I-40.

Bubba was a unique character.

As we drove down the highway he offered up a chorus of hymns and myriad worship songs over the CB radio waves, testifying of God's goodness and mercy that had been demonstrated in his life. I heard many expletives come back across those radio waves from *pagan* truckers bitterly offended that Bubba would use those channels as means to preach about his Jesus. But that didn't phase Bubba one bit. If anything, it only fueled his passion for this Jesus he spoke so zealously about. Bubba knew something, I could tell. He struck me with a strange combination of spiritual oddity and unbridled kindness. He was a little weird about his faith, but at the same time it intrigued me. He came across as someone who knew what he believed and why he believed it. It made him secure. I wanted that kind of security that I felt in his presence. But I didn't want some creepy religious thing to happen to me.

Bubba asked me if I was hungry. I hadn't eaten anything in nearly three days. I wasn't just hungry, I was famished. I was so skinny by this time I only had one stripe in my pajamas… I could hang-glide on a Dorito… I had to run around in the shower to get wet… You get the picture!

Bubba pulled off the interstate and into the parking lot of a Pizza Hut that advertised a buffet with an all-you-can-eat sign on the window. Those words on the sign made me salivate. My eyes swelled up like Wile E. Coyote in a Road Runner spotting. My stomach slowly began to expand like a boa constrictor anticipating a catch. I think I even began to pant a little.

For the next two and a half hours, I owned that buffet and Bubba owned my attention. In what seemed to be a thousand times, I went up, filled my plate, came back to the table, sat down and listened to Bubba talk about Jesus, all the while gorging myself with this unbelievable manna from heaven with tomato sauce and pepperoni spread atop. I was happy stuffing myself and he was happy to have someone to share his Jesus with. This may have been the most meaningful two-hour co-dependent relationship in history! I wasn't going to interrupt Bubba by no means; I was hungry. And Bubba sure wasn't going to stop me from eating; I was listening.

Amidst the gluttonous dosage of stuffed crust and mozzarella cheese I managed to devour that night, Bubba had some interesting things to say.

He told me of a time when he was addicted to heroin and showed me some scars on his arms. He pulled out a picture and showed me what he looked like while he was *using*. The photo made Sasquatch look like a clean-cut poster child for everyday hygiene products. Bubba looked like some kind of mutant, rabid bear in the photo. He had carried this picture around with him for years as a simple reminder of what his life looked like before Christ transformed him and set him free from his addictions. He certainly looked different. And his charisma had me spellbound during our time together.

We got back into his truck that evening and journeyed a few more hours together into North Carolina. With each mile marker that passed, I heard another eulogy of honor come from Bubba's mouth ascribing praise to the goodness of God. I listened with inquisition. Is there really a God? And, if so, does He have a good thing planned for my life? I wondered reservedly as I listened.

In the middle of the night, Bubba pulled into a rest area for a siesta. He let me sleep in his comfortable mattress in the back of his cab while he slept cramped up in the front seat. After spending many cold nights on the streets, that tiny bed in the cab of a rig seemed to me the honeymoon suite of a five star hotel in the Caribbean. I slept like a baby.

The next morning, Bubba and I said our goodbyes. He was headed eastward and I was going northbound toward Maryland. Before he let me off to begin my hitchhike north on I-85, Bubba gave me a list of churches in Maryland that he wanted me to consider checking out once I got to my destination. I sensed that this man was somehow connected to something much larger than just a trucking industry. He seemed to be part of, well, something much bigger than life itself, like some kind of *holy* mafia or angelic network that protected vulnerable teenage runaways from a cruel and dangerous world. And when I read Hebrews 13:2 years later, I'm not so sure I wasn't being *entertained* by an angel in Bubba. I know that hell has her angels of mischief, but I'm convinced through my journey in life that heaven has her angels at work in this world too!

That brazen truck driver's generosity and kindness left an enduring mark on my life. I wasn't ready to look further into this Jesus of his at that time, but a small seed had certainly been planted in my heart.

Bubba was a faithful witness to his God, and one day I'll see him in heaven. What excites me most about seeing Bubba again one day is for him to discover that his labor of love wasn't in vain. He didn't see this fourteen-year-old helpless teenager come to Christ through his effort that day, but he planted a seed of kindness... a seed that would eventually grow into a genuine relationship with Jesus. He was the hands and feet of Christ in that moment. One day he will find out that the teenager he reached out to grew up to become a Christ-following giant slayer.

I've never seen Bubba again in my lifetime but I'm looking forward to reuniting with him one day in heaven and sharing some "Giant Slaying" stories together over none other than some great Italian pizza! What would be more fitting?

I managed to arrive in Maryland several days later. I made it to my aunt's house safely to the shock of everyone in my family. I spent about a month there before a mediator worked with my parents to fly me back to Florida. After being away from my family for so long and having *proved* that I could runaway and survive, I felt I had some bargaining power to get my dad to stop beating me the way he did. This small step of independence, gave me a sense of empowerment that I could now leave anytime I wanted to escape my father's rage. I no longer had to stick around and be his punching bag, I could take measures into my own hand and simply take-off. This gave me confidence to go back home and try to work things out with my family.

I really did want things to work out. I loved my family. But at the same time I could also sense the resentment, anger, and rebellion that was being fostered in my heart, and especially the hatred I began to feel toward my dad. And now with this newfound sense of independence from running away and making it all the way to

Maryland from Florida at fourteen-years-old, this had the making of a very dangerous combination.

As I sat on the plane back to Florida, I pondered what things would look like once I got back home. Would things begin to change? Could my father and I learn to get along? Would we ever become a normal family? Would I be treated like a human being or continue to be kicked around like an unwanted dog who isn't necessarily valued, but legally bound to the real estate.

I also struggled with the feeling of having lost my mother. I missed her so much. Sure she was still alive, but my father had taken her away from me, obliterated her from the picture all-together and manhandled my life like I was some kind of rag doll. I could no longer get to her. He stood between us like an insolent fourth-grade bully blocking the entire hallway making sure no one could pass through. She was always in a distant shadow anymore. It made me reminisce of the old days when he wasn't around. It was so much better having an absentee father than an abusive father. At least in the former state, I had my mother. But this *13-foot giant* now stood between her and me.

Would I ever get my mother back? I pondered this from 30,000 feet as I looked out of the compact window of the airplane down on the world below. Do I belong down there in that vicious world? It has been such a cruel place for me thus far. Does my life really have a purpose? Is there meaning down there? Was Bubba right? Is there a God who can make sense of all this pain and suffering?

The landing gear engaged and we touched down at Tampa International. Life felt so surreal, and safe, at 30,000 feet looking down. Now that we had landed and returned to the jungle, I was afraid...

Chapter Four
When All Hope Is Lost

One of the best safeguards of our hopes, I have suggested, is to be able to mark off the areas of hopelessness and to acknowledge them, to face them directly, not with despair but with the creative intent of keeping them from polluting all the areas of possibility. ~ William F. Lynch

I don't believe my dad liked being violent. I have come to learn more about his heritage in my adult years that sheds further light on what made him tick.

My father was also subject to abuse as a child, yet he always spoke of his father with the utmost of admiration. He adored his dad. I never really understood that, especially after some of the stories I've heard from other family members documenting the alcoholism, sexual abuse, and maltreatment that went on in his lineage. Generational curses are ugly giants. And the demons of abuse; whether physical, verbal, psychological, or sexual, don't just go away without a fight. They are merciless giants; ruthless menaces invading ancestries for decades. For this generational curse to be slain, it would take a more powerful being to come in, bind up the strong man, and deliver a deathblow that would bury the tyrant in a *13-foot coffin.*

The only man strong enough to do that was a bloodstained warrior who came back from the dead two thousand years ago after being unjustly executed on a wooden cross; a cross that had been reserved for outlaws and convicts.

Every story has an author and an assassin.

My father wasn't the assassin in my story. He had only been carrying around the dark demons from previous generations that he didn't know how to break free from. He wasn't the enemy; although, in the eyes of a physically battered teenager, he was the antagonist. And as my body began to get bigger and develop physically, I would begin to stand toe to toe with my dad and fight back. The domestic violence and physical altercations that would ensue started to look like ultimate fighter cage bouts. From my angle, our home felt like a gladiator coliseum with combatants walking around on pins and needles every second of the day just waiting for an aggressor to instigate a clash. Even when things were quiet it was as if we all knew there was a sleeping lion in the arena that would eventually awaken with an appetite for blood and carnage.

I tried my best not to be home alone with my father when my mother and siblings weren't around. I knew from experience that he typically unleashed his most violent flurries when there was no one around to witness the melee. So I tried to stay out with friends and be active as much as possible. But it was just a matter of time before the inevitable happened. And when it happened, it was vicious.

After a knock-down-drag-out fight with my father one Friday night that resulted in me getting hit with an obscure object, I ran away again. Only this time I wasn't going to waste my time hitchhiking. I stole my father's *Volkswagen Beetle* and justified my actions by telling myself he made me do it through his cruelty. Plus, he had left the keys in the ignition; a temptation I couldn't resist that came with an extra spark of revenge.

This is the seed of a victim-mentality.

It gives birth to full-blown self-justification in every choice we make. If we can convince ourselves we are the victims in every situation then we can justify any and every response, no matter how irresponsible it may be. My wife and I have had a ministry to juvenile offenders for nearly twenty years now and we've seen this mindset in incarcerated kids all across the country. If I am the victim, then I am justified in stealing anything and harming anyone who stands in my way. I know what I am doing is wrong, but because I am a victim I have been forced into this lifestyle of "getting mine" before someone else "gets me." It may just sound like an old worn-out cliché, but two wrongs never make a right.

At fifteen-years-old, before I even had a driver's license, I stole my dad's Volkswagen as a means of getting away from my father. I drove it about forty-five miles to Gainesville where the engine blew. It had an old *slick-shift* gearbox and I didn't know how to change the gears. I'm surprised it made it that far. So I left it on the side of the interstate and started hitchhiking, again. This time I was going to go to Maryland and never come back to Florida again, I resolved.

My Life "Up In Smoke"

I managed to get a lift from a couple of *Cheech and Chong wannabes*, or so it seemed. They introduced me to marijuana and we were all "up in smoke" before the day was through. I felt myself casting off all moral restraint. I began to view life through the lens of a *what-the-hell* attitude. Life was becoming exceedingly meaningless, helpless, and annoyingly ambiguous. My life was being reduced to nothing more than surviving techniques. And I didn't even know how long that would last.

My *Cheech and Chong* look alike friends dropped me off at I-10 where I hitchhiked east to Jacksonville. From there, I caught a ride with a young entrepreneur who was heading to Savannah, Georgia, for a business meeting. Blaine was the proprietor of a bicycle shop in Jacksonville who at one time had been a homeless teenager.

Blaine's story fascinated me.

His parents had divorced and his custodial mother turned into a drug addict. He left home when he was fifteen. Fending for himself, he slept under bridges, fed off of restaurant scraps given to him by local restaurant workers, and lived primarily off the streets in Jacksonville. With all the odds in the world stacked up against him, this fellow managed to survive a homeless youth, eventually met a mentor who helped him get his G.E.D., and later went into the U.S. military. After serving his country, he came back to Jacksonville and began his own business, a bicycle shop on the beach.

I found his story to be nothing short of amazing. This man had come back from extraordinary odds and made something for himself. Amidst my perilous circumstances as a runaway teenager, I got a very small snapshot of hope; that a life of success and meaning was perhaps possible – even for me. But this snapshot would be more to me like a fleeting photo that landed in my hands and quickly blew away with the winds of reality.

Blaine had a hotel room reserved in Savannah. That evening he let me crash in his room and get a much-needed hot shower, an amenity I hadn't had in over a week. The next morning our paths would part. Blaine handed me a business card with his name on it and urged me to look him up one day when I got my life all straightened out. I obliged and made my way back out to the interstate to resume my hitchhiking journey to Maryland.

A couple of days later, I got to my aunt's house in Baltimore. This time, my relatives weren't as surprised to see me as my previous runaway the year before. It's almost as if they were expecting me. They notified my parents of my arrival and my parents notified the authorities. Before the evening had ended, I had been picked up by the police, taken to a juvenile jail cell for a few hours, and then escorted to a state-appointed foster home.

This wasn't part of my plan – living in a foster home with a couple of other misfit teenagers, who not only had *issues*; they had *subscriptions!* I didn't come all the way to Maryland to be placed in a stranger's home. I came to be rescued by my relatives. But my dad was going to make sure that my relatives; especially those on my mother's side had no influence or proximity in my life. He saw them as a threat to his tyranny over my life, and he could control my fate better if they weren't in the picture.

I was in the foster home for about two months. During my stay there I was educated by my peers in the *art* of smoking weed, staying up late watching violent movies, sleeping all day, and shoplifting from the nearby retail store in our spare time. And our spare time was the time we weren't smoking weed, watching violent movies, or sleeping. In my estimation, I was better off at my aunt's house. One day, after I got into a fight with one of the boys at the foster home over an argument about cigarettes, I took off and found my way to my aunt's house about thirty miles away.

My aunt's house and my grandmother's house were the only places in the world where I felt safe. But even now, I had grown tired and weary of the constant struggle – the endless running, the unrelenting tussle to survive, the overwhelming challenge of holding out for the dawning of a better day, and the disheartening conclusion that my father would always make my life not just miserable, but hopelessly oppressed.

I felt like giving up.

The Suicide Solution

All the running away could never make a permanent difference in my life. It only gave me a temporary reprieve. I couldn't go on like this forever. And going back to Florida and facing my giants there was not an option. For the first time in all my plight, I had lost all hope. I felt completely helpless and powerless. "Things will never change," I told myself as I reached for the pills in the medicine cabinet.

That night I planned on ending it all.

I would wait until the next morning when my cousins were at school and my aunt was at work, and I would take all the prescription pills I could find, and unconsciously fade into some kind of eternal paradise at best, and at worst, just a state of ceaseless non-existence; oblivion… but at any rate, I would be free.

Circling my mind like a marquee were the words of another Ozzy Osbourne song: *Suicide Solution.*

> *You can't escape the master keeper*
> *'Cause you feel life's unreal and you're living a lie*
> *Such a shame who's to blame and you're wondering why*
> *Then you ask from your cask is there life after birth*
> *What you saw can mean hell on this earth*
> *Hell on this earth!!*

My life was hell on earth and it couldn't get any worse. So in my assessment, any existence or non-existence in the hereafter would be a better alternative to my present existence. I was ready to jump ship and terminate this life here on earth. To my recollection, this was the first time I every prayed.

"I don't want to die, but I have no reason to live," I cried silently. "God, please take me to heaven if there is such a place."

I penned a brief suicide note and then took out about twelve bottles of pills; all the prescription meds I could find throughout the house, and sat down on the sofa to begin my journey into the unknown. I swallowed each pill methodically one after the other as I watched an Oprah Winfrey episode on the television. "Oprah's got some messed up guests on her show, but their lives aren't nearly as messed up as mine," I boasted to myself with the last taste of twisted humor I could muster out of my soul.

Ingesting the last pill, I lay back on the sofa and waited to sink into a state of oblivion. In a little while, I'll be free…

I vaguely recall hearing my aunt walk through the front door of the apartment and crying out as she suddenly noticed the empty pill bottles all over the coffee table. The last thing I remember was looking up at two medics hovering over me as they wheeled me into an ambulance. I spent the next four days in the ICU as my body wrestled, beyond my control, with the notion of staying or leaving.

The doctors pumped my stomach several times while a priest and two nuns had come in to pray over my soul, I would later learn. My mother immediately caught a flight from Florida and spent the ensuing days at my feet in the hospital room. When I began to regain consciousness a few days later, my first glimpse was of my mother sleeping at the foot of my bed. It was in that moment I realized how much pain I would have caused her if my plans had succeeded.

As I write this chapter near 25 years later, I can't imagine the joy I would have forfeited if my life were terminated at fifteen; looking across the room at my beautiful wife of fifteen years now, a charming nine-year-old daughter who is a state champion gymnast, an awesome seven-year-old boy who I like to call *Taekwondo Dude*, and another beautiful little four-year-old princess who I presume will be the first female linebacker to ever play in the NFL! Having founded an organization that gives hope to thousands of at-risk kids and underprivileged children every year, I can't imagine having missed all of this; a life of purpose… a life of beauty… and a life of empowerment for others. I'm dancing with destiny today, but it all could have been wiped out and so many countless lives would've been affected, if my attempt to take my own life had been successful.

I had come to such a dire place of hopelessness that I didn't think anybody would miss me if I were gone. My mother pulled herself up to my bedside, looked me straight in the eyes and said, "Promise me you will never do anything like that again."

Still in a groggy stupor, I promised.

But that still didn't take away "Goliath" in my life. He was still in Florida… and once again, I would be getting on a plane and going back to the Sunshine State to somehow try and find meaning to my life. I was still in a state of shock, astounded to be alive. I thought for sure that when I took all of those pills it would be over. And now after seeing my mother's pain from my near fatal suicide attempt, I knew that I could never again attempt to take my own life. This "Nuclear Option" had been taken off the table. Running away was getting old. Killing myself was out of the question.

What else could I do?

MTV Hopes and Spandexed Dreams

As the plane touched down once again at Tampa International, this time I wasn't entirely alone. My mother was sitting next to me and that offered me a small dose of hope… a little reassurance that I hadn't yet lost her completely.

But I needed more than a dose of hope to avoid my father's explosive outbursts. I needed a plan of action. Something that would keep me busy and out of my father's line of fire as much as possible.

One of the things that kept me busy was a rock band that my friends and I started my junior year of high school.

Intruder was the metal band we started in a friend's garage, and like every other garage band in the universe, we had our sights set on being on MTV one day. I played drums for *Intruder*. At first, we sounded a lot like the *Wyld Stallyns* from the movie *Bill and Ted's Excellent Adventure*. But as George Carlin would say, "They do get better."

Our band began by playing at parties and other small venues around town. We even landed a gig at the Elk's Lodge where the local senior citizens did most of their socializing. That one was set up by the good intentions of my probation officer; the one assigned to me for stealing my dad's car. We played on a chicken plucking stage in the parking lot of the lodge. It didn't go so well. We found out quickly that Black Sabbath and senior citizens don't mix. We didn't develop much of a fan base at the Elk's Lodge. But my probation officer did manage to get me a dishwashing job at the lodge that helped me stay out of my dad's terrain when I wasn't elsewhere with the band.

We had a much better turnout at a concert we did at our high school. To this day I still have the VHS tape of that performance, if you dare to call it such. Playing in front of three hundred screaming groupies gave us a little ego… well, a *big* ego to be more accurate. We believed we were on the track to heavy metal stardom. "One day Van Halen will be opening for us," I smugly announced to my English teacher in front of the entire class. "I know bands that have been split up for ten years who are still trying to pay off the debts they incurred from their music ambitions," she snapped back. "Not us, Mrs. Spaid, we are going to make it," I argued.

If you find grammatical errors in this book, now you know why; I was always disrupting English class with my heavy metal musings.

Mrs. Spaid was a very gentle-spirited teacher. Her quiet strength reminded me a lot of my grandmother in a younger frame. She often talked about God in class, even using Bible passages as examples for her students to analyze different kinds of styles and structures of literature. Her demeanor was a pleasant fusion of humor, compassion, and authentic concern for people. She really cared about her students. Her class was my favorite. And I'm sure she would get a chuckle at the irony of hearing that her wanna-be-rock-star-class-clown of 1987 didn't grow up to be a *rock god*, but rather, a Christian author and ordained minister.

As Irvin S. Cobb observed, "Humor is merely tragedy standing on its head with its pants torn."

It wasn't often that I thought about God as having a sense of humor during my adolescent years, but when I did it was usually during Mrs. Spaid's English class. She brought a different perspective to life and pain. And I desperately needed a fresh perspective on the wounds I had been carrying around in my soul.

The band scene had me hanging out at parties every weekend. Our hair grew longer and the spandex pants got tighter! I started to get involved with a rather dicey crowd. Drugs, alcohol, and promiscuous behavior were only the surface of the trouble that I would start to find myself in.

It was responsible of my parents to want to monitor my shady associations and to limit my activity with the band. They could tell I was getting into some dicey crowds. I was beginning to flirt with a pursuit of vanity that, left unchecked, would have me rumbling down a dead end street of futility and peril, and worst case, prison time. But I had already lost all respect for my father and wasn't willing to see him as my ally. None of his guidance could be construed as wholesome in my life after all of the physical, emotional, and psychological trauma he had caused me. I was bigger and stronger now, I could defend myself if he tried to assault me, and in my judgment, I didn't have to answer to him. I was my own man at sixteen-years-old and I could do whatever I wanted.

Arrested Development

I had adopted the mentality that the world had dealt me a bad hand so any of my transgressions weren't morally wrong, only justified responses to a world that wanted to hurt me. I've seen this same mentality in thousands of youth offenders locked up in juvenile centers all across this country as I travel and share my story. This narcissistic mentality brought about a hardening of my heart. I became calloused, learning to shut down emotionally, suppress my conscience, and not care about people or my actions in hurting them. When I wanted something, I just went out and took it. Whether it was walking into a shoe store, putting new shoes on my feet and walking out, or breaking into a warehouse to steal things we needed for our band, I had no value for other people's property. Because life had dealt me a bad hand and delivered the blows I had been given, anything goes – and everything is justified. "That's how the world works," I told myself.

Friends of mine had broken into our high school and stole some equipment from the band room. I ended up buying some of the stolen items from them fully aware that this was *hot* merchandise. I didn't care; I just wanted to enhance my drum set. Eventually, an investigation brought about my involvement and I was indicted in the crime. But I wasn't going to stick around long enough to be prosecuted.

I ran away again, but this time I wasn't leaving the state. I was too involved with the band. Over the next month and a half I hopped around from house to house, staying with different friends each week. Sometimes I slept in vacant houses and had friends bring me food when needed. I didn't want to risk being seen in public during the day, knowing the authorities were searching for me and had a warrant out for my arrest. But I felt safe coming out at night.

One night our band was playing at a nightclub when an undercover police officer showed up looking for me. He threw handcuffs on me inside the club but I managed to break free as we went out the front door. I ran into the woods and tried to hide. I couldn't get very far with my arms lodged together in the cuffs. My heart pounded, shooting waves of adrenaline through my body as my fight-or-flight responses instinctively kicked in and I took cover behind a fallen tree. I nervously peaked over and saw the officer panning the area with his flashlight. I tried to remain as still as possible, hearing the leaves rustle with the officers movement. The rustling became crisper with each step the officer took, closing in on my hiding spot. "Please don't let him find me," I prayed silently in my heart.

Before I could *think* the word "amen," the officer yanked me up by the arm, pulled me out of the wooded area and escorted me back down to the parking lot to his car; me tussling with him every step of the way. Backup officers had arrived on the scene and they helped the arresting officer put shackles on my feet so I couldn't run again.

I was caught.

No more running. No more hiding.

I was taken to the Hernando County jail in Brooksville. There I would be booked, fingerprinted, and promptly transported to the Marion Regional Juvenile Detention Center in Ocala.

The police car drove into a fenced area with barbed wire all around it. As the officer pulled me out of the car, a very large woman stood at the jail entrance. *"It's kinda hard to run in them-there shackles… they have the tendency to trip you up,"* she taunted me in her southern vernacular. I anticipated her spitting a wad of dip out of the side of her cheek, but I think she saved it for later.

She was a peculiar jail guard, but she couldn't have given a more anesthetizing assessment of my present situation. I had become numb.

At about 3:00 in the morning, my transport van arrived in Ocala at the juvenile detention center. I was checked in, given a pair of state clothes, and assigned a six-foot by eight-foot cell. My bed was a concrete block with a mattress about three-inches thick. The rusty toilet sat about eight-inches from the bed. It smelled like a sewer pit. I was cold… very cold. As I lay down on the mattress, I started to shiver as I began to ponder what my life would look like in the morning.

Did it even matter – the life that I would wake up to? What kinds of people are locked up in this joint anyway? Was this the end? Would I ever see any of my friends again?

I certainly didn't want to see my family again… at least not my father. He was the villain in all of this. He was the reason I was now in this pit of despair. Or, so I rationed.

And what about this God I had been hearing about from Bubba and Mrs. Spaid? If He is real, why did he allow me to end up here?

Somewhere in another "galaxy" far away, my precious grandmother was on her knees praying that God would save her grandson. She took a hold of the golden horns of the altar and wrestled with God. She knew that if God didn't intervene soon, I would end up dead or in prison.

She prayed... and she prayed fervently. I would later read a story that Jesus told in the Bible that reminded me of my grandmother:

> And he told them a parable to the effect that they ought always to pray and not lose heart. He said, "In a certain city there was a judge who neither feared God nor respected man. And there was a widow in that city who kept coming to him and saying, 'Give me justice against my adversary.' For a while he refused, but afterward he said to himself, 'Though I neither fear God nor respect man, yet because this widow keeps bothering me, I will give her justice, so that she will not beat me down by her continual coming.'" And the Lord said, "Hear what the unrighteous judge says. And will not God give justice to his elect, who cry to him day and night? Will he delay long over them? I tell you, he will give justice to them speedily. Nevertheless, when the Son of Man comes, will he find faith on earth?" (Luke 18:1-8 ESV)

Grandma kept coming. She kept praying. She kept interceding.

And God was about to answer her prayers! A miracle was on the way.

Chapter Five
The Prodigal

The glory of God is man fully alive. ~ *Saint Irenaeus*

I knew a man once who said, 'Death smiles at us all. All a man can do is smile back.' ~ *Maximus (from the film Gladiator)*

The Roman gladiator was an ancient phenom.

The word *gladiator* means "swordsman" and derives its meaning from the Latin word *gladius* ("sword"). The gladiator was an armed combatant who entertained audiences in the Roman Republic and Roman Empire in violent confrontations with other gladiators, wild animals, and condemned criminals.

Some gladiators were volunteers who risked their legal and social standing, not to mention their lives, by appearing in the arena. Most were despised as slaves, schooled under harsh conditions, socially marginalized, and segregated even in death. For Romans, "gladiator" would have meant a schooled fighter, sworn and contracted to a master. Irrespective of their origin, gladiators offered audiences an example of Rome's martial ethics. As the last event of the day, the gladiators who were condemned to death were brought into the arena as a spectacle for the excited crowd, were put on display in barbaric fashion, and found that by fighting well, they could inspire admiration and die with honor. And in some cases, even win their freedom.

In 1 Corinthians 4:9, we see some powerful imagery that Paul uses to illustrate our faith journey:

"For I think that God has exhibited us apostles as last of all, like men sentenced to death, because we have become a spectacle to the world, to angels, and to men." (1 Corinthians 4:9 ESV)

Without question, Paul is here referring to the gladiatorial games of his day and comparing himself and his fellow companions of the faith to the Roman gladiators of his day. I love Moffatt's translation of this text. He says, "God means us apostles to come in at the very end, like doomed gladiators in the arena!"

The word "spectacle" in this text comes from the Greek word *theatron*, which refers to a theatre, or public show in which a man is exhibited to be gazed at and made sport of.

I think Paul's big idea is this: in the theater of life, and especially in our faith journey, we don't get to choose the arenas we are thrust into. But at the end of the day, when the main event takes center stage and we have this death sentence hanging over our lives as we go toe-to-toe with spiritual adversaries, we *do* ultimately get to choose *how* we will fight. And by choosing how we will fight, we determine the honor that will become part of the redemptive story of our lives – honor that indeed belongs to the very author and perfecter of our faith; Jesus Christ.

Gladiators don't get to choose their arenas, but they do get to choose *how* they will fight. We don't get to choose our giants, but we do get to choose *how* we will face them; engaging them with uninhibited courage, or sulking in dreadful fear.

Young David didn't go looking for a giant to slay. But when he found himself thrust into the arena of fate, he didn't flinch. He went out one day with one agenda: serve and meet the needs of other people; and in *servanthood* he wound up getting caught up in a dance with destiny. He didn't let other people define who he was or what he would become. His older brother, Eliab, was jealous of his boldness and presumed to know the "evil" intentions of David's heart. He judged David wrongly, attacking the very integrity of his motives, solely because he envied the courage that David had, that Eliab himself should've had.

Isn't it interesting that sometimes the harshest attacks we face in life come from within our own household? Our deepest wounds often come from those of our own bloodline. In my life, the deepest wound in my soul came from my father… being abandoned by him in childhood and later suffering extreme verbal and physical abuse from him in the most pivotal years of my adolescence.

For David, the wound came from his oldest brother. The verbal attacks came but David didn't allow them to define him. He had a dance with destiny – a giant to slay, and glory and honor to bring his God. He couldn't afford to let anyone, including someone of his own household hold him back by trying to define his life.

God would later say of David that he was *a man after God's own heart*, drawing a distinct contrast to how Eliab tried to smear him. David didn't let Eliab define him; he let God alone define him. As a result, a giant nearly ten-feet tall came tumbling to the ground that day and as Goliath's remains promulgated the glory of God throughout all of Israel, and a *13-foot coffin* has testified of this triumphant overcoming-all-odds story throughout hundreds of years now.

I wonder what kind of impact our lives could have on this planet if we let God alone define who we are and what we were made for – not our adversaries, not our giants, not those who have hurt us, not even our own self-esteem, but God alone. Imagine what our lives could be if we let Christ alone define us…

A Defining Moment

Sitting in the Ocala juvenile detention center, I wasn't thinking too much about God's definition of my life, I was more obsessed with how I could break out of the joint.

The first three days I was there, I couldn't stop examining every crevice in the building for a means of escape. Whenever we were in the yard I discreetly inspected the barbed wire fencing, hoping to find a loop in the security. "First chance I get, I'm out of here," I convinced myself. I had seen *Escape from Alcatraz* and I figured if Clint Eastwood could do it, I could do it. I just needed to bide my time until any narrow margin of opportunity afforded itself.

That was my plan… until a gray-haired preacher sauntered in and messed up everything!

It was *Day Three* of my incarceration when Preacher Woody came to the juvenile center for his weekly visit. What I didn't know at the time is that this man would one day become a redemptive father figure in my life.

Preacher Woody was a unique man who overflowed with genuine love for kids. He strolled into the rec room where about sixty youths were seated and waiting for the commencement of his "church" service.

I observed him very closely, watching as he set down his bags of literature and methodically went from one youth to the next, greeting them by wrapping his arms around them in a very genuine expression of affection. "How can that man hug those criminals?" I asked myself. *"He doesn't even know what those cons were doing last night. I do, and if he knew, he wouldn't be embracing those scheming sinners like that."* I watched this man rove the room and greet every single youth as if they were the most important person on the planet.

I was mystified.

A few minutes later, this juvie-evangelist set up a 16mm film projector and started a movie called *A Long Way Home*. It was a *Gospel Film* taken from a story in the Bible about the Prodigal Son (Luke 15). It's the story of a boy who takes his father's inheritance, runs away to a far off land, and squanders the inheritance on reckless and wasteful living. Having spent everything, the young lad feels a sense of remorse. What's more, he realizes that he is wasting his life away when, in light of his father's abundance, it is completely unnecessary.

> "But when he came to himself, he said, 'How many of my father's hired servants have more than enough bread, but I perish here with hunger! I will arise and go to my father, and I will say to him, "Father, I have sinned against heaven and before you. I am no longer worthy to be called your son. Treat me as one of your hired servants."' And he arose and came to his father. But while he was still a long way off, his father saw him and felt compassion, and ran and embraced him and kissed him. (Luke 15:17-20 ESV)

Have you ever been surprised by an act of compassion? Or taken aback by someone's unexpected gesture of kindness?

Think about this young man's dilemma. I know that my father has plenty of goods in his house to spare, but I'm not good enough or worthy enough to have it. I've wasted not only the inheritance that he spent years saving up for me, but I've also brought disgrace upon my father's very name and disrepute to his household. Certainly I've caused him enough embarrassment for a lifetime and been his greatest source of shame. I have failed him. I have dishonored him. I am his black sheep. He never wants to see my face again.

Guilt consumed – but grace beckoned.

It took unspeakable courage for this boy to arise, go back home to his father, and admit that he had failed. He no longer saw himself as worthy to be a son, but it was his childlike belief in his father's *goodness* that led him to believe he could at least be accepted back as a servant. What he would learn is that his father's goodness was even greater than he ever imagined. The father didn't just bring him back as a servant; as soon as he saw him in the distance, he stormed out of the house and ran down the road kicking up dust in his trails just to embrace his son. When the father got to him, he hugged him, brought him into the house, threw a party like never before, and celebrated that this son of his who was once lost, was now found.

As I watched this story unfold on the grime-matted, worn out projector screen hanging from the ceiling of that juvie center, I couldn't help but to recognize the stench of my own sin. I knew I had been the victim of needless abuse, but for the first time in my life I began to realize I was not just a *victim*, but I was also a *villain* in my own story.

Preachers would refer to this gnawing and pricking revelation as the *conviction of the Holy Spirit*.

It hit me like a ton of bricks; I had not only been running from a violent earthly father all these years but I had also been running from an inexhaustibly gracious Father in heaven, whose goodness over my life was far greater than anything I could ever imagine.

This would come to be the defining moment in my life; I made a conscious choice to not let any other person, sense of failure, internal hurt, painful experience, fear, guilt, or injustice done to me, ever define who I would become. God's *love* alone would come to define Jimmy Larche for the rest of his journey on this earth and the afterlife to come. I would come to be defined solely by my heavenly Father's love for me and His goodness toward me. I didn't understand what all of that meant in the moment, but I knew something supernatural was happening in my heart.

The supernatural begins to take shape in our lives when we realize the greatest giants we will ever face are the villains inside of us. Usually they come in the form of pride, arrogance, spiritual rebellion, self-will, or the infamous "feel sorry for myself" syndrome: the victim mentality. These inward villains kill us from the inside out. We must learn to slay the victim mentality. You are the worst villain in your own story. When you begin to own this and take responsibility for your life, grace goes to work on your behalf and amazing things start to happen.

Scripture says there is none righteous, for all have sinned and fallen short of God's standards (Romans 3:10). We can't go around blaming someone else or the injustices done to us for what our lives will ultimately become. We must realize that the worst enemy we will ever face is the *enemy-in-a-me.* When we face this enemy, acknowledging our rebellion toward God, and surrender to the grace of Jesus, God draws near to us, bringing purpose to our lives, meaning to our stories, and the right interpretation to our suffering.

Peter warns us that God opposes the proud but gives grace to the humble (1 Peter 5:5). "Draw near to God, and he will draw near to you. Cleanse your hands, you sinners, and purify your hearts, you double-minded," exhorts James, the brother of Jesus (James 4:8).

When we take one step toward the Father's house in admitting we have sinned, He storms out of the house and pursues us with irresistible grace, kicking up dust and rocks along the trail as He runs to meet us. It won't be long before we find ourselves in the Father's house celebrating his goodness and steadfast love for us. And it is in the Father's house that we learn that *our best days are ahead of us!*

That one step toward the Father's house will require an act of courage. It will definitely cost you some pride and surrender, but in that humility it will reward you with unimaginable peace and abundant life that Jesus wants for you (John 10:10).

When the movie was over, Preacher Woody stood up front and talked about Jesus like I had never heard before. "Jesus was a friend to sinners," he said. Then he spoke of the cross. I listened intently as he described the pain, agony, and torture that Christ suffered as he went to Calvary.

"The wages of sin is death," the preacher said emphatically. "But the free gift of God is eternal life" (Romans 6:23), he assured graciously, yet confidently.

This wasn't about bad news, it was all about Good News!

He had us all read out loud and in unison, John 3:16; "For God so loved the world, that he gave his only Son, that whoever believes in him should not perish but have eternal life."

As he spoke, it became clearer to me that Jesus suffered and died on the cross for my own sin. Suddenly, the crucifixion had become my doing. I had always assumed that Jesus died for a good reason, maybe a good deed, or that he was some kind of martyr of religion. But I had never understood it was for my personal sin that Jesus went to the cross. Could I have been the one who nailed him there? I wasn't even alive two thousand years ago, and yet I'm beginning to feel a personal sense of responsibility for this immortal event that all of history and eternity is shaped around. It wasn't merely the Roman soldiers who hammered the nails into his flesh or pierced his brow with thorns. I saw the hammer in my hand. My sin crucified Jesus. And the amazing thing is, he didn't have to absorb my sin. But it was his steadfast love for me that kept him on the cross when at any moment he could've called down more than twelve legions of angels to rescue him.

I held the *hammer*, but he wielded the *forgiveness*.

Why did he do it?

> For our sake he made him to be sin who knew no sin, so that in him we might become the righteousness of God. (2 Corinthians 5:21 ESV)

God, the Father, sent his sinless son to die on the cross so that Jesus could take all of our sin and shame upon himself; exchanging his goodness for our sin, so that we could be made acceptable in God's sight. That's where mercy, grace, and justice come in. Justice is getting what we deserve. Justice must be served or God is *not* good, he is merely lenient and can therefore be bribed with evil, deceit, or manipulation. His holiness demands justice. That's what makes God perfect and *good*. So God takes the punishment we deserve and puts it on his son, Jesus. This means the penalty has been paid and justice has been served. Mercy is not getting what we deserve. We deserve punishment for our sins, the wages of sin is death, but we don't receive eternal condemnation because Jesus takes the "rap" for us. Then grace steps in and gives us what we don't deserve: the free gift of forgiveness; peace with God, a fresh start, and eternal life.

It reminds me of a story I once heard about a small boy who was consistently late coming home from school. His parents warned him one day that he must be home on time that afternoon, but nevertheless he arrived later than ever. His mother met him at the door and said nothing. At dinner that night, the boy looked at his plate. There was a slice of bread and a glass of water. He looked at his father's full plate and then at his father, but his father remained silent. The boy was crushed. The father waited for the full impact to sink in, then quietly took the boy's plate and placed it in front of himself. He took his own plate of meat and potatoes, put it in front of the boy, and smiled at his son. When that boy grew to be a man, he said, "All my life I've known what God is like by what my father did that night."

Just like the father in the story, God removes our plate of sin and all of its shame, and replaces it with Jesus' plate of forgiveness, fullness, and abundant life (John 10:10). Show me a better deal in the universe and I'm buyin'!

It all comes down to one simple choice: receive this free gift that God offers. Accept his plate of forgiveness.

How can you receive it? I'm so glad you asked. Because when you make this decision, you will be slaying the biggest giant you will ever face in your life: the giant of spiritual rebellion.

Spiritual rebellion looks at God and what Jesus did on the cross and screams out in arrogance, "I don't need You or your gift." Rebellion leaves us to our own demise, leading to nowhere but destruction. "There is a way that seems right to a man, but its end is the way to death," Psalm 14:12 warns us.

We can end our spiritual rebellion and get off the path to destruction by one simple, yet life-changing choice: surrender to Jesus!

That's what I did that night in juvie. When Preacher Woody led us in a prayer, I simply said in my own words:

> *"God, I'm sorry. I know that I've hurt you and I've sinned against you. Right now, I accept this free gift of life that you want to give me. I believe Jesus died in my place on that cross. Forgive me and*

come into my heart. Help me to live for you the way you want me to. Amen!"

It really was that simple, and when I prayed that prayer it felt like the weight of the entire world had been lifted off my shoulders. A very small seed of faith had been planted in my heart. It needed to grow, but a new life had supernaturally been conceived. There would still be many difficult trials and difficulties to come, but I was no longer alone.

New Beginnings

Preacher Woody visited the juvenile center once a week, and sometimes twice a week. Every time he visited, I had countless questions about God, the Bible, and Jesus. Each week he loaded me down with new books and literature to read. It was like Christmas every time he visited. He delivered the goods and I obsessively delved into everything he gave me.

Just like David and those Roman gladiators, I hadn't chosen my arena in life. I didn't choose to be abandoned as a child. I didn't choose to be callously abused by my father later in my youth. And though my actions may have led to my arrest and incarceration, I didn't choose to get locked up. But getting locked up was the best thing that ever happened to me.

I didn't choose this arena, but one thing was clear: I had been given a new beginning and a fresh start through my relationship with God, and like the gladiators, I could choose *how* I would fight from here on out.

I was scared to go home at first. A couple of weeks after my defining moment, I went before the judge and he was going to send me home on house arrest. But I didn't think my faith was ready yet. I was afraid that going back home would make me vulnerable to my father again and that I would somehow screw it up and end up on the streets again. I just wanted to sit in juvie for a while and continue studying and soaking up the Word of God. I know it sounds absurd, but juvie became my first seminary. It's where I began to study the scriptures adamantly. And the Word of God was changing my heart.

The rest of the juvies thought I was crazy. The judge was going to send me home but I refused? "What's wrong with you?" one fellow inmate chided me after we left the courthouse on the transport back to jail. One of the corrections officers looked on in dismay. He said he had never seen anyone do that before in the history of juvenile courts.

"Awesome! I made history," I told them.

Three weeks later, we went before the judge again and I told him the same thing, "I don't want to go home." I even wrote the judge a letter stating that I wanted to be placed in a foster home; a *Christian* foster home with Bible-believing parents. I was truly a new person and I didn't want anyone or anything to mess it up. I didn't trust my father or myself enough to go back home, only to see the whole cycle of violence start back up again. My heart was new, and I wanted my surroundings to be new.

What I would have to learn is that we don't always get to choose our arenas. But we can learn to fight differently, and we can learn to fight well... for Jesus, in whatever arenas he places us in. I also learned that God would never put us somewhere or place something on us that he didn't think we could handle.

> No temptation has overtaken you that is not common to man. God is faithful, and he will not let you be tempted beyond your ability, but with the temptation he will also provide the way of escape, that you may be able to endure it. (1 Corinthians 10:13 ESV)

I didn't get my wish. My petition to be sent to a Christian foster home was denied by the judge. Instead, he sentenced me to a short-term offender program, better known as S.T.O.P. Camp. I would spend a couple of months at Stop Camp, a wilderness work release program, and simultaneously obtain family counseling so that I could gradually be assimilated back into my family. I accepted it as God's will for me. It was inevitable: I will have to go home sooner or later and face that giant all over again. I must begin to believe that God has a plan in all of this and that I must build my faith so that I can be ready to face the moment when it comes.

Until then, Stop Camp would be my "boot camp" to strengthen my faith.

Spiritual Boot Camp

One of the worst parts about Stop Camp was *Maggot Patrol*. Every Monday, our "chain gang" would rummage through dumpsters to rescue aluminum cans for recycling. In the process, we would often come across maggots and other wonderful critters, thus the name *Maggot Patrol*.

Stop Camp worked us like I had never worked in my life. At first it was grueling, but in time I came to appreciate the work ethics I was learning and the disciplines it was producing in my life. In the evenings we played ping-pong, cards, and enjoyed relaxing conversation around the campfire.

One of my highlights every week was when Mr. Tim showed up for Bible study. I told him about Preacher Woody and how my life had been changed in juvie. He made contact with Preacher Woody and the two would often come out to Stop Camp together.

Every Tuesday night, Mr. Tim brought us cookies and other snacks. Some of the boys came to chapel only for the cookies, but that's okay, they heard the Word anyway. Just like my experience with Bubba the truck driver in that Pizza Hut, God's Word will not return void. It will go forth and accomplish its purpose, even if kids come out to chapel merely for the snacks. They will leave at least thinking about what they heard. I don't care how or why they come, when exposed to the Word of God, they always walk away with a spiritual tension that must be resolved.

I scavenged on the Word of God at Stop Camp like I had feasted on pizza that night with Bubba at the buffet. I devoured everything Mr. Tim brought. It was like manna from heaven. Mr. Tim always brought a boom box with him and we learned to sing the same praise choruses they sang at his church. I assure you the harmonies weren't as pretty, I know we made some hounds cry in the woods on the outskirts of that camp, but my spirit was being fed and my faith was growing. This was important. I would need all that I could get before I went home.

My parents visited Stop Camp frequently. The visits were civil but the real test would come when I came home for good. I was hopefully optimistic about returning home and trying to be a witness to my family, and especially an agent of grace toward my father. I knew my life had changed, but had it changed enough? That seemed to be the all-consuming question that I wrestled with; did I have what it takes to go home and forgive the person who had been liable for inflicting the deepest wounds in my soul?

I took great comfort in the Word of God. While other campers took advantage of movie nights at Stop Camp, I utilized that time for studying the scriptures. I started reading Billy Graham's book *Peace with God*. It pointed me to a passage in the Book of Romans that I meditated on often:

> Therefore, since we have been justified by faith, we have peace with God through our Lord Jesus Christ. Through him we have also obtained access by faith into this grace in which we stand, and we rejoice in hope of the glory of God. More than that, we rejoice in our **sufferings**, knowing that suffering produces endurance, and endurance produces character, and character produces hope, and hope does not put us to shame, because God's love has been poured into our hearts through the Holy Spirit who has been given to us. (Romans 5:1-5 ESV)

It was starting to make sense to me. Everything that I had ever suffered as a child was part of God's plan to produce something good in my life. He was building a person of endurance, character, and boundless hope. As Mr. Tim taught us the story of Joseph in the Book of Genesis, I could sense that much like Joseph's past, all the misfortune in my life was being used to bring me into a life of purpose, destiny, and meaning.

I read in Jeremiah 29:11, "For I know the plans I have for you," says the Lord. "They are plans for good and not for disaster, to give you a future and a hope" (NLT). And the first verses I ever memorized apart from John 3:16; "Trust in the LORD with all your heart and lean not on your own understanding; in all your ways acknowledge him, and he will make your paths straight" (Proverbs 3:5-6 NIV).

It had become unmistakably clear, God knew my past, and He was in control of my future. For the first time in my life, I felt secure. I finally had what Bubba had; peace.

Blaise Pascal once wrote:

> "Either Christianity is true or it's false. If you bet that it's true, and you believe in God and submit to Him, then if it IS true, you've gained God, heaven, and everything else. If it's false, you've lost

nothing, but you've had a good life marked by peace and the illusion that ultimately, everything makes sense. If you bet that Christianity is not true, and it's false, you've lost nothing. But if you bet that it's false, and it turns out to be true, you've lost everything and you get to spend eternity in hell."

Life is about risking everything for what you believe in. And I have found that there is nothing in this life more liberating than faith in Jesus. My relationship with him has brought meaning to my past, belief in my now, and hope for my future.

One of my favorite movies to watch with my kids is *Cheaper by the Dozen 2*. We get a lot of laughs out of this film. I love the closing statement just before the credits roll on the screen:

> *"You have to settle with the past, engage in the present, and believe in the future."*

This is what happened to me as a result of getting locked up in that juvenile detention center. The old had passed; the new had come (2 Corinthians 5:17).

The story of my life now had a brand new beginning.

Chapter Six
Getting Past Your Past

I would rather die a fighter than survive with a victim mentality.
~ Jimmy Larche

So baby dry your eyes
Save all the tears you've cried
Oh, that's what dreams are made of
'Cause we belong in a world that must be strong
~ Dreams by Van Halen

Theoden: I will not risk open war.
Aragorn: Open war is upon you whether you would risk it or not.

Great theological truth from the film *Lord of the Rings*!

From the moment we are born into this world, we are thrust into an arena of epic warfare. As I write, there is a spiritual battle being waged over your soul and everything God has destined for you to become. As we saw in the previous chapter, gladiators didn't get to choose their arenas, but they did get to decide how they would fight – and to what honor they would give themselves.

"I am a soldier, I fight where I am told, and I win where I fight," General George Patton brashly proclaimed.

We don't get to choose our battlegrounds, but we can control *how* we choose to fight. Every brutal assault on our life makes us either *bitter* or *better*. If we are to fight well for God's honor, we must decide to let our giants make us better. We can't allow the pain or suffering of our past to release toxins into our present and future.

We do have a choice.

I Am David is a film adapted from Anne Holm's internationally acclaimed novel *North to Freedom* and is one of my sentimental favorite movies. It's about a twelve-year-old boy who escapes a communist concentration camp in Bulgaria sometime after WWII where he has spent nearly his entire life. He sets out on a risky journey across Europe trying to reach Denmark in hopes of finding freedom, facing imminent danger and uncertain people along the way. Because he grew up locked in the camp while suffering mindless cruelties, severe injustices, and daily abuse, he is emotionally calloused and doesn't trust anyone.

It becomes a spiritual voyage of discovery where David slowly loses his instinctual mistrust of humanity and begins to smile, share, trust, and ultimately, love.

This film awakens so many emotions in me; eerily taking me back to that psychological prison my father had me in for so many years.

David depicts the resilient, unbreakable spirit of a youth who overcomes traumatic circumstances and insurmountable odds to experience restoration, redemption, and a stirring reunion in the end. Perhaps the most touching scene in the movie is a conversation about *trust* that David has with his new friend, Sophie.

> David: Why do people do such terrible things?
> Sophie: Like what?
> David: Like beat people, and kill them, and make them prisoners.
> Sophie: Most people don't do that, David.

David: My friend Johannes always used to tell me, "Trust no one."
Sophie: Oh, life wouldn't be worth living if you did that, David.

So many people never experience David's kind of resiliency – resiliency that leads to freedom, peace, and a fulfilled life; a life that can only be found by learning how to forgive, love, and trust in *goodness* once again. So many people choose to remain in that emotional prison. Having been hurt by another person's cruelty, they spend an entire lifetime carrying around hurts and toxicities from their past, releasing them into other relationships everywhere they go. Unfortunately, many of the people who never get past their past end up continuing a vicious cycle of inflicting pain on others.

Hurt people hurt other people… unless their hurts are properly healed.

There's a relatively short, yet fervent prayer in the Bible that serves as an encouraging response to those who have found themselves suffering through pain and hurts caused by others. The first book of Chronicles briefly depicts a well-respected man named Jabez (ancestor in the lineage of the kings' tribe of Judah) whose prayer to God for a *blessed* life was answered. The author pauses in this genealogy to give Jabez a place of honor in a long list of Kings and their lineage.

> Jabez was more honorable than his brothers; and his mother called his name Jabez, saying, "Because I bore him in pain." Jabez called upon the God of Israel, saying, "Oh that you would bless me and enlarge my border, and that your hand might be with me, and that you would keep me from harm so that it might not bring me pain!" And God granted what he asked. (1 Chronicles 4:9-10 ESV)

The name Jabez means "he causes pain," so we can assume that something about his birth was exceptionally more painful than the usual birth – either physically or emotionally. In Bible times, a name was very important. A name often defined a person's future and what they would become. So perhaps Jabez's mother was predicting her baby's future.

It seems as if Jabez defied his hopeless name and dysfunctional beginning to become a man who believed fervently in the power of God. He prayed with urgency and vulnerability. He cried out to the Lord with boldness! His relationship with God must have been exceptionally noteworthy to cause the author of Chronicles to stop and elaborate on this one man's life.

Though Jabez's story began in pain, he believed it didn't have to end that way. He prayed that God's blessing, rather than pain and sorrow, would come to define his life – and God answered! Jabez grew up to become a respectable man of God with an enduring legacy of honor. I believe that when he prayed for God to keep him from harm, he was not only praying for God to protect him from suffering future hurts, but also to prevent him from living out of his pain and causing other people pain.

Maybe you need to stop right here and pray a simple prayer like that one:

> *"God, keep me from suffering further harm, but also keep me from living out of my hurts and thus hurting others."*

What a respectable prayer!

I sometimes wonder what my childhood would've looked like if my father had prayed that prayer after his father had hurt him. I'll never know the answer to that, but one thing I do know: by *owning* my pain, my children's lives won't suffer from the generational curses that were passed down through my father.

There have been numerous accounts circulated by other family members of generational abuses rampant on my father's side of the family. It would stand to reason that because my father never found healing in getting past abuses he suffered, he in turn inflicted recurring abuses on others, primarily my mother and me. People who don't heal, sadly, return the misfortunes of cruelty on others in the same manner it was inflicted upon them. They never learn to love because they've never learned to live from grace.

If we don't own our pain, it will own us, and we will inevitably hurt others in our journey. By owning it, we surrender our *victim mentality* to Christ, allow God's healing to bring new life into the mix, and we start living from grace rather than the hurts that once owned us. This is the "blessed" life that Jabez experienced. Jabez could learn to love because of what he lived out of. He lived out of faith in God's redemptive purpose rather than the reverberation of his pain.

And we can too!

In *The Sacred Romance*, John Eldredge wrote, "At some point we all face the same decision – what will we do with the Arrows we've known? Maybe a better way to say it is, what have they tempted us to do? However they come to us, whether through a loss we experience as abandonment or some deep violation we feel as abuse, their message is always the same: Kill your heart. Divorce it, neglect it, run from it, or indulge it with some anesthetic (our various addictions)."[iii]

Nothing kills the heart more subtly than unforgiveness.

Forgiveness Is Not An Option

I read somewhere that *unforgiveness* is like lighting yourself on fire and hoping the other person dies of smoke inhalation.

When we don't forgive, we allow our giants and villains to have power over us even long after they are no longer in our lives. Without love and forgiveness, there is no resiliency to the harms done to us. Ann Landers once said, "If you have love in your life it can make up for a great many things you lack. If you don't have it, no matter what else there is, it's not enough."

If we are going to follow Jesus with reckless abandon, slay some giants along the way, and build an enduring legacy of honor, love is indispensable. Without it, we will fail miserably, regardless of all the good intentions we may have. There is no real freedom without love and forgiveness. Period.

There are no shortcuts to recovery.

The road to recovery is paved with one decision after another to forgive, heal, and keep pursuing your God-inspired dream while intentionally leaving the toxins of bitterness and resentment behind. I had to learn this as I prepared to leave Stop Camp and go back home to face my giants. My father would be waiting for me and forgiveness was not an option. This was the cross Jesus commanded me to take up for his sake.

The night before my release date, I read a story in Matthew 18 where Peter questions Jesus about how far one should be willing to go in forgiving someone else. Like any good preacher, Jesus answers the question with a story:

> Then Peter came up and said to him, "Lord, how often will my brother sin against me, and I forgive him? As many as seven times?" Jesus said to him, "I do not say to you seven times, but seventy times seven. "Therefore the kingdom of heaven may be compared to a king who wished to settle accounts with his servants. When he began to settle, one was brought to him who owed him ten thousand talents. And since he could not pay, his master ordered

him to be sold, with his wife and children and all that he had, and payment to be made. So the servant fell on his knees, imploring him, 'Have patience with me, and I will pay you everything.' And out of pity for him, the master of that servant released him and forgave him the debt. But when that same servant went out, he found one of his fellow servants who owed him a hundred denarii, and seizing him, he began to choke him, saying, 'Pay what you owe.' So his fellow servant fell down and pleaded with him, 'Have patience with me, and I will pay you.' He refused and went and put him in prison until he should pay the debt. When his fellow servants saw what had taken place, they were greatly distressed, and they went and reported to their master all that had taken place. Then his master summoned him and said to him, 'You wicked servant! I forgave you all that debt because you pleaded with me. And should not you have had mercy on your fellow servant, as I had mercy on you?' And in anger his master delivered him to the jailers, until he should pay all his debt. So also my heavenly Father will do to every one of you, if you do not forgive your brother from your heart." (Matthew 18:21-35 ESV)

It became very clear to me that I couldn't avoid forgiving the person in my life that was responsible for the most pain in my world. I had to separate my will from my emotions. I had to realize that forgiveness was an act of the will, not a feeling. I didn't feel like forgiving anyone. But I had to choose to be free. We cannot control our feelings, but we can control how we choose to respond despite our feelings being what they are. Not too many people enjoy the process of forgiving, but that shouldn't deter us from making the tough decisions that will free our soul from deadly toxins.

Unforgiveness is really trying to take the easy way out – the path of least resistance. At best, it's spiritual laziness because it lets feelings rule without being challenged by our real beliefs and the tough teachings of Jesus. At worst, it's flagrant disobedience to God

– a blatant sin that pushes Jesus further away while clutching to the harbors of prideful rebellion. Either way, unforgiveness yields the same bitter results and causes us to pay a terrible price in the end.

Forgiveness is never easy, yet I have learned over the years that it can be appropriated and celebrated more intentionally when I break it down into steps:

1) Acknowledge the pain. Sin hurts. Sin is injustice. It is wrong. It grieves God and us. Own it by acknowledging the feelings you have.

2) Seek grace: ask God to help you by the power of His Spirit to make a real commitment of your will to do His will. If you really want to obey Him, then He will empower you.

3) Ask God to forgive you (for judging them or delaying obedience in forgiving): believe that He has and gratefully receive it.

4) Choose to forgive them: pray it and say it by an act of your will; put your heart in it.

5) Choose to forgive yourself (for prolonging the pain): accept it. Then release the pain.

6) Pray for them – all of the blessings you would like God to bestow on you. Then watch how God returns blessing on your life.

7) Choose to believe God's promise of redemption over your life (Romans 8:28). Rejoice in it and *celebrate* it. Now go treat yourself to some ice cream!

At times, nothing can be harder than choosing to forgive. But in the end, there is nothing more liberating than forgiveness. The question is: How bad do you want to be free? How desperate are you to begin a journey in becoming fully alive? This is where God beckons you… where the Spirit calls… and where Jesus walked. Will you follow him?

To this day, my father has never owned his hurts inflicted upon me, nor has he ever apologized. Which makes forgiveness all the more challenging. One of the most difficult things God has ever had me do is look my unrepentant father in the eyes and tell him, "I forgive you." I didn't feel like forgiving him, and he certainly didn't merit it, *but I made the toughest decision one must ever make in taking a step toward becoming fully alive; I chose to forgive.* It wasn't an emotion. It wasn't even reciprocated by any reconciliatory actions on my father's part. But it made a world of difference for me. I chose to face the bully, not run from him. I faced him with the unbridled confidence of a young David standing toe-to-toe with a seasoned Goliath. And as vulnerable as it was to look a bully in the eye and utter those words of grace, I walked away opening a whole new chapter to my life; one that would now be written in the ink of forgiveness, inscribed with the pen of healing, hope, mercy, and love. I chose to value my father as a person whom Jesus loved and died for, not as the villain he had been in my story; even though he didn't reciprocate the sentiments. Nothing to this date in my life has been more empowering.

In no way would the wounds of my father go away overnight. They would still emit emotional and psychological scars I must deal with for years to come. *But I had taken the single-most difficult step toward recovery one can ever take: release the villain, forgive the giant, and slay the victim-mentality.*

Too many people never find fullness of life because they aren't willing to look the giant in the eyes and say those words, "I forgive you." Instead, they relegate to coping skills that involve covering up the pain rather than dealing with it. Melissa Stewart cautioned,

"Consider your mind valuable, high rent property; and screen your tenants very carefully!"

When you refuse to forgive, you allow unwanted intruders to take up space in your soul; that villain is still there taking up real estate in your mind and in your heart. They can still intimidate you. Even if they are years and miles removed from your life, they can still *own* you. But when you release the villains through forgiveness, they can no longer own you. You are owned by a greater *cause* and liberated by the same spirit that brought Jesus back from the grave. The *Resurrection* and *Life* rolls a heavy stone away from your heart.

Take that tough step today to release a villain in your life and watch the amazing victory that God births in your spirit. Stop reading and do it right now!

Smashing TVs and Virgin Mary Statues

On February 4th, 1988, I walked out of Stop Camp, looked back and told myself I'd never be back in this place again. I think God must've chuckled. I've heard it said that if you want to make God laugh just tell Him your plans. His plan would later bring me back to this camp over and over again, and telling my story in hundreds of juvenile centers all across America. But that's for a later chapter.

I was on my way home and determined to make this homecoming much different than any of the others when I had run away. I was determined to *honor* God in my family. I was convinced that my whole family would soon come to know Jesus, and that would change the game for good.

Unfortunately, things don't always work out the way we hope or imagine.

When I got home from Stop Camp, it was halfway through my senior year in high school. If I had any hopes of graduating on time, I had to take day classes and night classes to make up for lost ground. I gave myself diligently to schoolwork, a part time job doing landscaping, and going to youth group on Wednesday nights and church on Sunday.

Preacher Woody went well out of his way to connect me with a local youth pastor, Terry, who could mentor me and help me get plugged into a church family. Coincidentally, Terry was a former rock musician and drug addict who also came to faith in Christ through Preacher Woody's ministry. Seven years prior, Terry went to a youth rally one night with no interest in spirituality. He had only hoped to get a date with the girl who invited him. He had a bag of marijuana in his pocket and wanted to get high with the girl after the rally. But similar to my story, that night he saw a faith film that convicted him of his rebellion and need of a Savior. After the film, Preacher Woody prayed with Terry and helped him begin a spiritual journey in following Jesus. Terry instantly got planted in a church where he was discipled for several years before becoming a youth pastor in Spring Hill, Florida, where we met.

I looked up to Terry a great deal. He was a huge inspiration to me. Our paths had been so similar and we shared a common bond with Preacher Woody, a spiritual father to both of us. Terry was a fiery youth leader. For me, the most memorable message he ever taught was one on idolatry. That night he used several props and object lessons of things we worship in place of God. He went on a holy rampage like that of Elijah and began smashing all these idols with a baseball bat, including an old forty-inch television set and a statue of the Virgin Mary. He shredded posters of "metal-head" rock gods in spandex pants. He didn't burn any books or CDs that night, but it still lit a fire in our souls.

Some people may say that Terry was extreme. But his message captured our hearts: with Jesus – it was all or nothing (Luke 14:26-27, 33). And God was serious about the commandment to have no other *gods* before him. D.L. Moody rightly charged, "You don't have to go to heathen lands today to find false gods. America is full of them. Whatever you love more than God is your idol." But in our culture we have a different label for someone who takes these words of Jesus literally: an *Extremist* or a *Radical*.

In American evangelicalism today, we prefer a *safe* God who doesn't call us out of our comfort zone; one we have tamed and fashioned after our likeness rather than One Who calls us to *His* likeness. Then we can't understand why there is no more dangerous wonder to our faith. In his book *Crazy Love*, Francis Chan says, "God doesn't call us to be comfortable. He calls us to trust Him so completely that we are unafraid to put ourselves in situations where we will be in trouble if He doesn't come through."[iv]

Consider A.W. Tozer's take on the *god* we have fashioned modern Christianity after:

> The God of the modern evangelical rarely astonishes anybody. He manages to stay pretty much within the constitution. He never breaks our by-laws. He's a very well-behaved God and very denominational and very much like one of us... we ask Him to help us when we're in trouble and look to Him to watch over us when we're asleep. The God of the modern evangelical isn't a God I could have much respect for.[v]

This isn't the God of the Bible; *one* we have managed to compartmentalize in our own little spiritual boxes and take out whenever we need a bailout or a rescue from crisis. Jesus' call to discipleship is black and white: all or nothing!

Dietrich Bonhoeffer soundly wrote, "Christianity without discipleship is always Christianity without Christ."[vi] And Terry's leadership modeled this truth. He taught me to understand the importance of following Jesus every day, not just resting on a faith decision that I had made in a juvenile center to save my hindquarters from a real hell. My salvation wasn't an "insurance plan" to keep me out of hell, it was the beginning of a long and difficult discipleship journey that God would use to shape me and conform me more to the likeness of His Son (Romans 8:29). This wouldn't be a *sprint*, it would be a *marathon*, and I had to train daily to learn how to run this race.

Something wonderful changes on the inside of us when we come to grips with the fact that God isn't after our comfort, He is after family resemblance.

His primary purpose in everything is to make us resemble more of Jesus. For us to become more like Jesus, we will have to take up our cross and follow him daily. And there is nothing comfortable about a cross! God will let anything and everything come into our lives for the ultimate purpose of making us more like Jesus. And Jesus didn't suffer so that we wouldn't have to; he suffered so that through suffering we would come to know him more intimately and be identified more with him in his likeness. Getting our way doesn't make us more like Jesus; it makes us more selfish. But pain, difficulties, and adversity demand us to cultivate spiritual disciplines, which in turn cause us to become more like Jesus in the long run.

Perhaps the most important thing Terry ever taught me was the discipline of having a daily quiet time with God; a time to search the Scriptures, meditate on God's Word, and learn to hear His voice. It was a routine of Jesus to rise early and pray before the madness of the day and the demands of the people were thrust upon him. And it was one of the first spiritual disciplines I must learn. "Deepest communion with God is beyond words, on the other side of silence," noted Madeleine L'Engle. If a time of silence and solitude to start the day was important for Jesus and his communion with the Father, how much more important it must be for us.

It wasn't easy at first, but eventually I found myself rising early each morning at 5:30am to have my quiet time before school and work. Whenever I missed that time with God, I could feel it throughout the day. John Bunyan said, "He who runs from God in the morning will scarcely find him the rest of the day." I found that to be true. What's more, I found that when I took the time to wait on God in the morning, even the busiest days (which are often the ones that compete with our quiet time the most) became not only more efficient, but also more fruitful in their labors. Relationships seemed to feel richer, opportunities were plainly realized, and decisions came with further clarity. It was like more work was accomplished with less effort. I think that's why Jesus gave us this great invitation in the Gospel of Matthew:

> Come to me, all who labor and are heavy laden, and I will give you rest. Take my yoke upon you, and learn from me, for I am gentle and lowly in heart, and you will find rest for your souls. For my yoke is easy, and my burden is light." (Matthew 11:28-30 ESV)

A daily quiet time with God is something I'm glad I learned early on as a follower of Jesus. It also helped me with my relationship with my father. By praying for him regularly I was able to find healing at an emotional level that was important for me to move in the direction of my spiritual destiny.

Graduating With *Honors*

June was quickly approaching and so was my high school graduation. It was a God-ordained miracle that I would be graduating on time with my class. Either that, or my teachers were very adamant about getting rid of me for good! I like to think it was the former.

A few weeks before graduation, I was walking down the hallway at school with a new t-shirt that had a picture of a door on the back with the words of Matthew 7:7-8, "Ask, and it will be given to you; seek, and you will find; knock, and it will be opened to you. For everyone who asks receives, and the one who seeks finds, and to the one who knocks it will be opened." A woman tapped me on the shoulder from behind and said, "I really like your shirt there, fella!" I turned around and almost stunned this woman into a blackout. It was Mrs. Spaid! It blew her away that Jimmy Larche, her former class clown and wannabe rock star, was wearing scripture. I just looked at her and said, "It's a long and crazy story, Mrs. Spaid, and I'll have to share it with you some time."

A few weeks later I graduated with *honors*…

Most of them were good friends of mine!

Honestly, there were days I never thought I would live to be seventeen, much less graduate high school… with my class for that matter. Our *Class of 1988* graduation song at Springstead High School was Van Halen's *Dreams*:

> So baby dry your eyes
> Save all the tears you've cried
> Oh, that's what dreams are made of
> 'Cause we belong in a world that must be strong
> Oh, that's what dreams are made of
>
> Yeah, we'll get higher and higher
> Straight up we'll climb
> Higher and higher

Leave it all behind
Oh, we'll get higher and higher
Who knows what we'll find?

As the gleaming red and blue graduation balloons lifted into the dusky sapphire sky of this little town on Florida's gulf coast, I felt a tremendous sense of accomplishment. I had not only graduated high school, but I had managed to live under my father's roof for the past five months without any incident of violent outbursts or hostility. I knew I would soon be moving on with my life. I had no idea what the future held for me. But for the first time since I was a little boy on a baseball diamond in Baltimore, I felt a tinge of childlike dreams being born again in my spirit.

I was free to believe. Free to hope. Free to pursue a life of significance.

The question is: Where do I start?

Though I didn't have all those answers yet, I was beginning to have my eyes opened to the reality that David's friend Sophie transmitted in the film *I Am David*; there are good people in this world and life wouldn't be worth living if you couldn't learn to trust once again. For me, that all started with learning how to love and forgive through the supernatural grace of God. And because of that, I found the freedom to dream once again.

Chapter Seven
Finding Purpose from Pain

God whispers to us in our pleasures, speaks in our conscience, but shouts in our pains: it is His megaphone to rouse a deaf world. ~ C.S. Lewis

The purpose exceeds the pain. ~ Beth Moore

Finding that one dance with destiny, that great purpose you were made for, is the most fulfilling joy in this lifetime and most important clue to interpreting the meaning of your pain. C.S. Lewis was right; nothing in the entire universe shouts louder than pain. It is God's megaphone in a deaf world. It is the pain, suffering, and injustices in our world that rouse the most tension in our hearts and move us toward a life of action and significance.

I was invited to a ministerial screening for the film *Soul Surfer* before it hit the theaters in April 2011. The movie is based on the true to life story of Bethany Hamilton, a thriving Christian youth surfer with great aspirations, who has her dreams shattered when she becomes the victim of a tragic shark attack, leading to the amputation of her left arm.

Amazingly, Bethany fights through unbelievable physical and mental challenges to get back on a surfboard only four weeks later, and ultimately become a pro surfer – with only one arm! There were two moments in this film that were captivating for me.

Here's the first:

Some time after Bethany recovers from her shark attack, she tries to get back on the board, admirably entering a surf competition with only one arm. The episode is extremely disheartening, leading to disappointment, frustration, and humiliation. With a dream to surf still wading in her heart, she feels helpless and powerless to move forward in the pursuit of that dream. She feels alone spiritually, abandoned in her faith, and thereafter begins to question the meaning of life. She's tempted to quit surfing altogether.

In this human struggle between a dream and a destiny, Bethany has questions and even doubts which are universal to us all:

Why did God allow this to happen?

Why do bad things happen to people who follow God?

How can I move forward when everything in my life has been shattered?

Does my life even matter anymore?

Bethany realizes that the greatest giant she needed to overcome wasn't that huge shark off the Hawaiian coast that severed her arm from her body; her greatest giant was self-pity. She must overcome that to become the warrior God destined her to be. Her dance with destiny was on the line. And God would use an unsuspecting event to open her eyes to all of this. She goes on a mission trip to Thailand with World Vision after it has been ravaged by a tsunami.

"I met so many courageous people who had lost so much but still retained hope for the future. It's a true inspiration to see people beginning the long road to recovery after such a devastating event," Bethany said.

On the trip she showed great humility, often saying to survivors, "I can't even imagine what you went through. I can only speak from my own experience." She had a touching moment with a girl who lost her mother and brother to the tsunami. Bethany was also instrumental in helping the tsunami survivors, especially children, overcome their fear of the ocean. She took fifty very excited kids from the village of Lam Tukkae for an afternoon of surfing at Patong Beach. For many of the children, it was the first time they had left their villages. They readily took to the water and surfing alongside of Bethany.

Her compassion, thrust into action amidst the pain and suffering of others, caused her to rightly interpret her own suffering. Bethany realized there was purpose to her pain. This teenage girl went on to realize her childhood dream of becoming a professional surfer, and has become an international symbol of bravery and determination for millions of people. But for Bethany, it wasn't her surfing that defined her; it was the *purpose* she discovered in her pain.

At the end of the film she tells a group of journalists that she has been able to *"embrace more people with one arm than she ever would've been able to embrace with two arms."*

That's what you call rightly interpreting your suffering!

Jesus didn't suffer so that we wouldn't have to suffer; He suffered so that through suffering we could come to know him more intimately and be identified with him more acutely in compassion for others.

But the other takeaway for me was this:

There was a time after Bethany first got back on the surfboard that others, including those closest to her, felt sorry for her disability. In their pity for her, they tended to lower their expectations for her comeback. But Bethany didn't appreciate their pity. She didn't want anyone to feel sorry for her or to fall prone to feeling sorry for herself anymore. She knew that a victim mentality wouldn't serve her "redemption story" well at all, and it certainly wouldn't slay any giants along the road to recovery.

On the contrary, she had a bitter rival surfer who never felt sorry for her.

In fact, her rival competed against her with dirtier tactics than ever before, never easing up on her one-armed opponent. And it was this opposition that gave her more grit and determination to overcome than any amount of pity she gathered from her sympathetic family and friends. Near the end of the film, Bethany realizes that adversity, even in the form of personal rivals, has a role in shaping our character and conformity to Christ. She looks her rival squarely in the eye, and with the utmost sincerity says, "Thank you for never taking it easy on me!"

Bethany is triumphant because she rightly interprets her pain, and she understands that adversity is here to make us *better*, not *bitter*. And her story continues to inspire thousands more each and every passing day. The film proves that suffering and tragedy doesn't have to define us. When the final chapter is written, our lives will be defined by how we respond to the suffering and hardship in our lives as well as our willingness to let God shape us in those painful chapters.

Adversity may be uncomfortable, but one day you will want to look your pain, suffering, or adversaries square in the eyes and genuinely say:

"Thank you! Your role in my life has been indispensable to my being conformed to the image of Christ. Your presence has given me greater purpose, greater character, and greater influence in the

world at large. 'Pain,' thank you for being a part of my journey. I wouldn't be what I am today without your companionship. I wouldn't love as much. I wouldn't have the compassion I have. I wouldn't feel what Jesus feels."

Now get back on that board *Soul Surfer*, you have a wave of destiny to ride!

God Never Wastes Our Suffering

I moved out of the house after graduation and before my 18th birthday. I had released my father as the villain in my life but I still didn't necessarily trust him. Callously unrepentant, he was still the same person and felt no need to change. I moved to Maryland to live with my aunt and begin college. My older sister had already moved out of the house before our senior year of high school after having strained relations with my father. A few months after I moved out, my younger half-sister ran away in the middle of the night and had her mother (my stepmother) send her a plane ticket to leave Florida and come live with her in Maryland. That left only my mother and my younger half-brother in the home with my father. And because my younger brother seemed to have an exemption when it came to my father's abuse, and the rest of the children were all gone, he began channeling his angst toward my mother.

My mother endured extreme verbal abuse from my father and frequent physical abuse over the next year and a half until she could take it no longer. She finally drew the line after my dad slapped her in the face in front of my little brother. She packed up and left the next day while he was at work, knowing that if she tried to leave while he was there it would get much worse.

The next day, I received a phone call from my dad out of the blue (he had never called me or reached out to me before). He sounded suicidal and told me he had a shotgun in his hand. I talked with him for about an hour and he eventually calmed down. I tried to explain to him that God was there for him, but he didn't seem all that interested in my faith. And though I felt compassion for this deeply wounded man, I didn't feel sorry for him. He had adamantly failed to own any wrongdoing in his life. A trail of bleeding and battered human beings were left in the wake of his rage, and it seemed that the only remorse he could muster up was solely for himself. I genuinely tried to offer spiritual guidance to him but it became clear to me he was only using our conversation to somehow relay hateful words to my mother, rather than find healing or some place of contrition. I feared from his verbiage that he would attempt suicide but I also knew I couldn't help a soul who continued to live in denial.

I continued to pray for him without having much contact with him since that day. We've seen each other a few times over the years. I even invited him to my wedding, and on each occasion I've been very intentional about extending graces toward him, but his heart seemed to get colder and more distant as years went by. Eventually I came to realize that just because I had forgiven my father, it didn't mean there would ever be much of a relationship there. Sometimes in life, reconciliation just doesn't work out even though you desire to be a peacemaker. It does takes two to tango. I've settled that in my heart over the years and have found perfect peace in *releasing* my dad over to God's stead.

For me, my best days were ahead of me and I would soon be a father myself. I had much to learn and much to rebound from. Even though I didn't have a great model of fatherhood in my biological father, God was faithful in giving me some great models of fatherhood in my mentor, Preacher Woody, and my step dad, Bob.

Your suffering comes at such a high cost. Don't waste it.

If pain comes at such an expensive tax on our hearts, we must allow God to redeem it for something of eternal value in this lifetime. All of us have a choice to make with our hurts – give them to God or harbor the resentment. When we surrender our pain to God, we learn to grow in grace and become life-giving channels of God's mercy, overflowing in the lives of other people all around us. God has put hidden treasures in our darkness. It is our part to seek out the value of our pain and invest it in shaping other hurting people in our broken world. This becomes the *cause* within you.

Jesus didn't suffer so that we wouldn't have to – He suffered so that in suffering we could come to know him more deeply. Jesus suffered constant rejection in his ministry, hostile threats from religious people, abandonment from friends, and the betrayal of one of his closest followers. This was all before the emotional and spiritual separation he felt from his Father as well as the violent thrashings he suffered at Calvary's cross. Jesus knew suffering well. The entire book of Hebrews is about a High Priest we have in Jesus who suffered like we suffer and *is intimate with our deepest pain.* He is familiar with our hurt.

> For I consider that the sufferings of this present time are not worth comparing with the glory that is to be revealed to us. (Romans 8:18 ESV)

As I write this book, a good friend of mine just suffered the loss of his second son. A little over a year ago, his 26-year-old son overdosed and was found dead in his apartment. On the anniversary of this tragedy, his 25-year-old son went out on the rooftop of a hospital, put a loaded pistol to his head, and pulled the trigger as police scrambled to reach him. He had written a lengthy suicide letter detailing his long battle with hopelessness, despair, and depression. He just couldn't fight any longer. He wasn't willing to stay in the battle. This young man gave up hope prematurely, and will never know the redemptive beauty of discovering the hidden treasure in his pain. He had succumbed to the deception in his heart, believing those lies that whispered, "You will never amount to anything."

It brought me back to my suicide attempt as a teenager and made me look at how demoralizing our suffering can be. Then I look at my life today and see the boundless *fruit* of hope, faith, and perseverance. For these two young men, they will never see the fruit of that hope; choosing to end their lives prematurely rather than hold onto the hope of a more redemptive chapter in life.

As I heard my friend read his son's suicide letter over the phone, I wept. I felt the pain. How much more does Jesus feel the pain? My friend had raised his children in a Christian home, taught them biblical values, and prayed regularly with his kids growing up. But the teachings of Jesus don't inoculate us from human suffering or immunize us from pain. Jesus didn't suffer so that we wouldn't have to. He suffered so that we, through suffering, could know him more deeply.

My friend must wake up every day and deal with emotions of grief, guilt, shame, and failure. The enemy wants him to believe that he failed as a parent. He will cause him to question the goodness of God. He will cause him to have doubts about his own personal faith in God. He will struggle daily with all the "what ifs" and ponder how the outcome could've been more favorable if only he had done something different. The giant of shame will tell him, "If you had played all of your cards right you could've somehow eluded all this pain. If only you had done this… if only you had been a better parent… if only you had sat down and had that one meaningful conversation and got through to your son… if only you hadn't said this or done that… if, if, if…"

This intimidating bully of shame and guilt must be slain.

No matter how well we play our cards, pain and suffering is a part of our journey in this fallen world. We don't get to control that.

Remember our gladiator friends? They didn't get to *choose* their arenas. They were brusquely thrown into them. But they did get to choose *how* they would fight… and that courageous decision was a direct attribution to the legacy they would die with, or the freedom they would ultimately win.

We all must make a conscious choice as to what we are going to do with our pain. For me, I couldn't spend the rest of my days paralyzed by fear, insecurity, and timidity because of my childhood distress. Nor could I cast off all restraint and live in irresponsible rebellion while blaming my father's abuse for my own actions. I wasn't going to adopt the victim-mentality and have a trump card as an excuse for my own failures. I decided early on that I would discover the rich meaning in my suffering and the hidden treasures of darkness buried in my pain.

It came at such a high price in my life; I wasn't going to waste it.

The World Ain't All Sunshine and Rainbows

There's a mesmeric scene in *Rocky Balboa*, the 2006 film starring Sylvester Stallone as underdog boxer of the same title. It's been thirty years since Rocky became the Philly phenom rising from inner-city obscurity to the ranks of heavyweight champion of the world. Now a retired widower living in Kensington, Philadelphia, Balboa owns and operates an Italian restaurant in the city called "Adrian's," named after his late wife. He decides to try his hand at one final match, ending up in an exhibition against the reigning champ. But his son, Robert, is struggling to find an identity on his own, and is growing weary of always living in his father's shadow.

They have a tense exchange outside of Adrian's restaurant where Rocky finally makes a breakthrough in his strained relationship with his son. After Robert (Rocky Jr.) unleashes a flurry of verbal jabs at Rocky about how difficult it's been being his son, Rocky comes back with a stinging uppercut of reality:

> *"Let me tell you something you already know. The world ain't all sunshine and rainbows. It's a very mean and nasty place, and I don't care how tough you are, it will beat you to your knees and keep you there permanently if you let it. You, me, or nobody is gonna hit as hard as life. But it ain't about how hard you hit. It's about how hard you can get hit and keep moving forward; how much you can take and keep moving forward. That's how winning is done! Now, if you know what you're worth, then go out and get what you're worth. But you gotta be willing to take the hits, and not pointing fingers saying you ain't where you wanna be because of him, or her, or anybody. Cowards do that and that ain't you. You're better than that! I'm always gonna love you, no matter what. No matter what happens. You're my son, you're my blood. You're the best thing in my life. But until you start believing in yourself, you ain't gonna have a life."*

If we are to live from a heart fully alive for God, one that makes a difference in the lives of others, shapes eternity, and leaves a lasting legacy on this planet, we must at some point in life come to a place where we no longer blame someone else for the life we now regret. We will have to cease pointing the finger at our villains, blaming them for all of our misfortunes, irresponsible behaviors, and lethal addictions. The reality is, we do have villains. And they hit hard. Life stuns us with painful blows. It's not pretty… it *ain't* all sunshine and rainbows. It *ain't* always pretty. But blaming people and making excuses only takes us further away from our dance with destiny. We must rise above the ashes of regret and begin to smell the fresh lilies of our dreams flourishing in an open field of God-ordained possibilities.

If anyone had a reason to shift the blame and sulk into a life of regret, it would be my mother. She gave birth to two children before she turned eighteen and had to drop out of high school to raise us while my father was still out sowing his wild oats with other women. Whenever he did come home it was a hostile environment where she suffered mindless abuses. The marriage was terminated when I was six-months-old. As a struggling teenage mother of two, Mom could've easily put life on cruise control, developed a victim-mentality, and anesthetized her pain through various addictions and dependency. But she didn't go down that road.

My mother went out and got her G.E.D., worked a day job and attended night classes at the community college while my grandparents helped out with raising us children. She was determined not to sulk into a "Why me?" attitude in life. She continued her education off and on over the next ten years until she decided to remarry my father. Mother believed that everybody deserved a second chance, and she gave my father the benefit of the doubt, believing he had grown up some since their teenage relationship. She also thought it was a constructive opportunity for her kids to have their father in the home. But things gravitated from bad to worse over the next seven years before she finally left him for good, once the children had all moved out.

For those seven years of my mother's second marriage to my father, her entire life was reduced to being a pawn in my father's custody battles with his second wife. The custody battles were emotionally draining and the legal fees were financially exasperating. And amidst all this hardship, she must suffer my father's endless cycles of abuse all over again. She felt reduced to something that was subhuman.

When my mother was finally liberated from that abusive relationship, she went back to college and got her bachelors in business administration at 39-years-old and attained her CPA license at forty-four. Today she is a successful professional who has worked as a CFO for major corporations and has helped many non-profits bring about redemptive causes for the poor, and in standing against injustices committed toward women and children. She also married my step dad, Bob; one of the most caring and generous people I've ever met in my life. Bob became a redemptive father figure in my life. The Bible says "God places the lonely in families; he sets the prisoners free and gives them joy…" (Psalm 68:6 NLT). That's precisely what God did when he gave us Bob – he gave us a refreshing new portrait of what a fully functional family should look like. His example of honor, sensitivity, protection, compassion, and nurturing love is unrivaled in a generation where so many fathers have checked out. God has an inexplicable way of restoring the torn images of our lives. He will always fill the wounded holes in our hearts with restorative hope and empower us with loving people if we are willing to learn trust all over again.

My mother has discovered that God never wastes our pain; our suffering can be redeemed into ministry opportunities to serve and comfort others who are in distress. And I love to tell her story. She can relate to our great "theologian" Rocky Balboa: *"You, me, or nobody is gonna hit as hard as life. But it ain't about how hard you hit. It's about how hard you can get hit and keep moving forward; how much you can take and keep moving forward. That's how winning is done!"* Life has its blows, but we don't have to be victims who develop a martyr-mentality and flounder in a sea of regret or complacency. We can get back up and do great things in life through the strength of Christ, whose grace is sufficient in every arena of pain, suffering, and hardship.

The Stories Worth Telling

I woke up this morning, stepped out on the front porch before the sun came up and saw a piece of paper that apparently had fallen out of my 9-year-old daughter's backpack, and was lying on the ground. I picked up the paper, which was dampened by the moisture from the morning dew, and read the memory verse she had written on it. It was just what I needed this morning:

> And let us not grow weary of doing good, for in due season we will reap, if we do not give up. (Galatians 6:9 ESV)

Everything you have ever experienced in your life: the pain, suffering, hurt, abandonment, abuse, betrayal, or _____ (fill in the blank), has brought you to this place and time for a purpose so much bigger than you. God is choreographing your dance with destiny and there is purpose in the pain. Every injustice ever committed against you, and every injustice you've ever committed is redeemable through the blood of Jesus Christ.

God doesn't want you to lose heart. You will forfeit so much if you give up. Your story matters to God and community. Never let the enemy convince you otherwise. Do not grow weary, friend; face the villain, slay the giant, bury the coffin! You were made for this challenge.

You don't have to sulk in regret while pointing fingers, shifting blame, or eluding responsibility. Take back ownership over your life and evict the bullies who condemn you and judge you. Now give ownership over to Jesus and watch your pain be transformed into a life-giving catalyst God uses to bring hope and comfort to countless lives.

Let me remind you, dear friend, what stories are worth telling…

Frodo and Sam are in Osgiliath. It's under evil attack. Frodo is becoming entranced by the power of the Ring and he appears incoherent as he staggers toward a Nazgûl. Seemingly resolved to give up on the fight to continue his mission, Frodo offers the Ring to the Nazgûl and nearly puts it on. This is when his good friend Sam comes to the rescue, pulls him away from the evil entity, and saves the story. They fall to the ground. An infuriated and delusional Frodo takes his sword and points it towards Sam's throat. After a few seconds Frodo comes back to reality, drops his sword and says, "I can't do this Sam." Sam's response is true not only of Frodo's journey, but also of your story:

> "I know. It's all wrong. By rights, we shouldn't even be here. But we are. It's like in the great stories, Mr. Frodo, the ones that really mattered. Full of darkness and danger they were. And sometimes you didn't want to know the end because how could the end be happy? How could the world go back to the way it was when so much bad had happened? But in the end, it's only a passing thing this shadow. Even darkness must pass. A new day will come. And when the sun shines, it will shine out the clearer. Those were the stories that stayed with you that meant something. Even if you were too small to understand why. But I think, Mr. Frodo, I do understand. I know now. Folk in those stories had lots of chances of turning back, only they didn't. They kept going because they were holding on to something."

Frodo then asks, "What are we holding on to Sam?" Sam holds out hope: "That there's some good in this world, Mr. Frodo. And it's worth fighting for."

Sometimes it feels like you don't have what it takes to finish your own story. It feels as if everything is wrong and "by rights," you shouldn't even be here. Heaviness comes over you. The scars remind you of how far you have come... but how far you still have to go. Evil is set against you. Hell is bent on destroying you. Adversaries have made your demise their personal mission in life. Friends fail you. Close friends betray you. Failures haunt you. Regret taunts you. And amidst the whirlwind of all this pain, your spiritual nemesis causes you to question the meaningfulness of your mission and doubt the redemptive value of your life.

Remember that the stories worth telling are stories of desperate measures; where "folk in those stories had lots of chances of turning back, only they didn't. They kept going because they were holding on to something."

This was Frodo's story. This is the story of the Bible. This is the story of Jesus in the Garden of Gethsemane. And this is your story.

It's in times like this we all need a *Samwise* – a trustworthy friend who can break through all the madness, love us through the doubtful times, and encourage us to finish our race.

Dear friend: Your story derives its value not despite your pain and suffering, but because of it. It's a story worth telling... and it's definitely worth fighting for!

Chapter Eight
Dancing With Destiny

*A sense of destiny is our birthright as followers of Christ. ~ Mark
Batterson*

*When you become consumed by God's call on your life, everything
will take on new meaning and significance. You will begin to see
every facet of your life – including your pain – as a means through
which God can work to bring others to Himself. ~ Charles Stanley*

Our dance with destiny begins with the people we serve.

I was in college studying to be a computer draftsman when I
first sensed God's calling on my life for ministry. When I speak of
calling, I'm not saying I was eating alphabet soup when the words
"Thou shalt go" mysteriously formed together. The words "Go and
preach the gospel" didn't appear on a billowing wave in the Gulf of
Mexico. And I certainly didn't have any dreams of biblical
proportion involving fat cows, skinny cows, or supernatural
hallucinations. There were no visions of angelic graffiti sketched
across my mind.

God's call came to my heart in a *still small voice* – more like a
gentle whisper; yet its burden carried the weight of a *Loxodonta
africana* elephant.

I would describe God's calling on your life as something you
can't escape the weight of. It's a God-inspired burden within you
that will not leave you just because you choose to ignore it. It takes
a hold of your heart and consumes you until you concede. You see

signs associated with that calling everywhere. When a calling is truly from God, it will carry an unrelenting aggravation with it until you yield to it. It becomes your *Field of Dreams* moment: "But until I heard the voice, I'd never done a crazy thing in my whole life."

This *voice* is where your dance with destiny begins...

When I first heard the *voice*, I remember thinking at the time, "God, you've made your first mistake. I don't have much to give. The only thing I know how to do is play the drums." And with my roots in heavy metal music, I knew only two volumes: loud and louder. I would be a nightmare for any worship leader to try and tame. But I knew God's calling on my life entailed serving others, and I had been invited to play in the worship band at church. So I accepted the ~~challenge~~ call!

Matthew Barnett, the founder of the Dream Center in Los Angeles, has a great take on discovering God's cause within you:

> Often the best way to figure out the cause within you is through the oldest method in the world: trial and error. In other words, if you're trying to figure out what God created you to do, just roll up your sleeves and start serving in cooperation with somebody else's cause. I cannot tell you how many times I encounter people who are clueless about their cause, but once they get involved in serving people – regardless of the nature of the service – God gives them situations or opportunities that instantly ring their bell.[vii]

We are all called to serve. It's the way God has fashioned us. We are all called to add value to other people's lives through our serving. We are not just here to find a career, make a living, pay the bills, and somehow slide through life without going bankrupt. We all have a dance with destiny that God himself choreographs to change other people's lives. He leads, but it is our responsibility to yield our lives to that calling.

I began to serve my local church by being a part of the worship team and through that servitude I began to learn more about my unique gifting. I found other areas of strengths I didn't recognize to be part of my hardwiring. But that's how God works; when we eliminate our excuses and begin to serve, not only are other people benefited, we learn more about ourselves.

Some people do not feel qualified for ministry. But God doesn't call the qualified – he qualifies the called. If he has called you, never let someone else determine your qualifications, including yourself. Don't let your own feelings of inadequacy decide whether or not you are qualified. You have been bought with a price and your life is not your own. Rise at your Master's command and lay down your life in reckless abandon to the cause within you.

An Idiot's Guide to Changing the World

Have you pondered the ragtag little band of misfits that God chose to entrust the greatest mission in the world to? The disciples of Jesus weren't very impressive on paper, to say in the least. Matter of fact, every one of them would've failed most of our modern church planting team assessment phases. The Bible even describes them as *idiots*: "Now when they saw the boldness of Peter and John, and perceived that they were uneducated, *common* men, they were astonished. And they recognized that they had been with Jesus." (Acts 4:13 ESV). The Greek word here for *common* is "idiotes" which is where we get our English word *idiot*. That's right; God deliberately chose a group of uneducated idiots and unlikely misfits to ensure that the most important message in the universe got delivered successfully – and that God alone would get the credit and the *glory*.

John Eldredge put it this way, "God needs to get a message out to the human race, without which they will perish... forever. What's the plan? First, he starts with the most unlikely group ever: a couple of prostitutes, a few fishermen with no better than a second-grade education, a tax collector. Then, he passes the ball to us. Unbelievable."[viii]

Why does God choose the most unlikely of people? To make certain that nobody robs him of his own glory:

> For consider your calling, brothers: not many of you were wise according to worldly standards, not many were powerful, not many were of noble birth. But God chose what is foolish in the world to shame the wise; God chose what is weak in the world to shame the strong; God chose what is low and despised in the world, even things that are not, to bring to nothing things that are, so that no human being might boast in the presence of God. (1 Corinthians 1:26-29 ESV)

God is not interested in your credentials. Frankly, he laughs at them. They incline us to brag more on ourselves rather than boast in the presence of God. He calls the unlikely, or the inadequate, to secure his own glory. We humans are too quick to take the credit for accomplishments. We like to think our abilities sealed the deal. Truth is, our gifts are nothing without God's presence and our strengths are futile without his power at work in our lives.

When God called Gideon to lead the Israelites into battle against the Midianites, he gave him one of the strangest battle plans in the history of war. He reduced an army of 32,000 troops down to a mere 300 soldiers. He took this inferior band of brothers and charged them to face an army of about 125,000 battle-tested, well-trained, superior enemy troops. And here's the kicker: he equips them with nothing more than torches and watering pots for weapons. Talk about an underdog story. The plan seems insane. Why does God do it this way? The Lord explains to Gideon, "The people with you are *too many* for me to give the Midianites into their hand, lest Israel *boast* over me, saying, 'My own hand has saved me.'" (Judges 7:2 ESV)

God won't give HIS glory to another!

That's why calling the inferior, the inadequate, the seemingly unqualified, and the most unlikely has always been part of his plan. He relishes taking people whom others would consider unworthy or incapable, and calling them to do something extraordinary, so that in the end no flesh can boast in his presence.

One of the greatest giants most of us will face in our lifetime is the paralysis that accompanies feelings of inadequacy. When God calls us, we *should* feel inadequate to a degree. If we don't experience some measure of feeling deficient then we don't have the bigger picture yet. It's been said that if your dream is small enough to accomplish on your own, then it's not big enough to have God at the center of it. I would agree. But when feelings of inadequacy lead to paralysis of action on our part, we have been intimidated by a giant that must be reckoned with. We all get into ruts and fall into spiritual inertia at times. Yet when our lives are characterized by chronic inaction or failure to serve in ministry because we feel inferior, incompetent, or unworthy, we have become prisoners of war. We are slaves to merciless giants.

Three Pennies and an Unbelievable Dream

Agnes Gonxha Bojaxhiu felt called to ministry as a young girl and went through ministerial training in Ireland and India. When she graduated from her training her heart was *on fire* with a burning passion to serve God and love people. One day she approached her superiors and announced, "I have three pennies and a dream from God to build an orphanage." Her superiors could not believe what they were hearing! After laughing at her, they said, "You can't build an orphanage with three pennies. With three pennies you can't do anything."

Agnes just smiled and replied, "I know. But with God and three pennies I can do anything!"

For fifty years this woman worked among the poorest of the poor in Calcutta, India. We know Agnes Gonxha Bojaxhiu as *Mother Teresa,* who endeared herself to thousands of people. She literally gave her life away in sacrificial love to others. Mother Teresa did not have the material things that many have today, but she had a passion and a God-inspired purpose; which gave her life meaning and direction. The impact of her love and kindness impacted millions around the world.

She only had 3 pennies and a dream that burned in her heart. That was enough! She felt the hand of God was upon her life and He would open up the way, and provide all she needed. Negative voices, or meager resources could not deter her. She would instead place the dream, and the passion, in the hands of God and let Him work things out for His glory. We can learn from that.

Let God be God!

Trust Him to be your provider, your guide, and your strength. Let Him work out the dreams that He has placed in your heart. He knows what's best! He knows how to bring it about! "He who calls you is faithful; he will surely do it." (1 Thessalonians 5:24 ESV)

Your life is too valuable to God and others to remain on the sideline. You are made to serve. You are designed to impact other people's lives. God invites you to co-labor together with him in shaping eternity and making heaven more beautiful. Don't settle with lame excuses any longer, and don't be restricted by the estimations of other people. When the devil tells you that you are unworthy for God to use, tell him, "You're right!" Then proceed to point the enemy of your soul to God's grace and remind him of how *worthy* Jesus is, and that this same Jesus lives on the inside of you. When other people tell you that you aren't qualified to do something great for God, tell them, "That's exactly why God called me. He doesn't have to worry about me robbing Him of His glory." Life is too short and eternity is too long to get trapped in ruts of inertia. You have a difference to make in someone's life. Get after it and let God get all the glory.

It's time to slay some giants!

After serving on the worship team, I began serving on the drama team at my church. This defied my instincts because my whole life growing up I was afraid of being in front of people. But God surrounded me with a group of wonderful people who helped me get beyond the fear of being on a stage. I didn't understand this at the time, but this season of serving on the drama team and worship team was vitally important in God's shaping me for my future dance with destiny. One day I would become a preacher and a national communicator of God's *Good News*. Yet the thought of public speaking at that time in my life was not only panic inducing; it was more the likes of a feeble toad being dropped into a pond swarming with famished water moccasins. I wasn't ready to become that prey. But it is in *serving* that we find clarity to the cause in our heart and the call of God on our lives. My youth pastor used to tell me, "It's easier to steer a car when it's moving than when it's sitting in the driveway." That came to be my motto in serving. As long as I was serving others, my gifts were coming to the surface. The dots connected more clearly.

My dance with destiny was being choreographed by serving others.

Learning from Coca-Cola

If you are struggling to find God's calling on your life right now, I would suggest that there's no better place to start than serving in your local church. I believe the local church is where God wants us to begin. Even though people have given up on the church, God hasn't. It's still his primary agenda for changing the world.

Today, the whole world knows about Coca-Cola. Some would suggest more of the world knows about Coke than it does about the Gospel. The Coca-Cola strategy for decades has carried this message: "Think globally, act locally." When I read this it reminds me of Jesus' *Great Commission* (Matthew 28:16-20) and the last objective he gave his followers (Acts 1:8). God has a global vision He wants us to capture and it all starts with serving the local church.

As I write this book, church attendance in America is at an all-time low. Yet in the same era, the rate of parachurch organizations being incorporated every month is astronomical. It's off the charts. I believe this depicts a generation eager to serve a cause, but flirting dangerously with abandoning the mission of the local church. I understand the church has failed in many ways and this generation has ample reason for being distrustful of the local church, but we cannot abandon her. Jesus isn't looking for a new mistress; he's interested in building a better bride. His bride is the church. And we must not give up on her in pursuit of our "more noble" global causes. Making disciples must be at the core of the cause we serve in as followers of Jesus. If it's not, then we aren't serving Jesus; we are merely serving a Christ-less *cause*, regardless of how noble it may be.

I'm certainly not opposed to parachurch ministries. My wife and I founded and have overseen a non-profit organization that works with at-risk kids and their families for over fifteen years now (www.breakawayoutreach.com). Through fierce advocacy, this organization has served underprivileged children, prisoners' kids, juvenile delinquents, inner-city students, and impoverished families. We run a ministry to Chattanooga area at-risk youth and foster an international network of like-minded ministries to youth around the globe. We *need* parachurch organizations that focus on specific people groups, special needs, and concentrated missions. But if these parachurch organizations are to serve the cause of Christ, they should work through and with the local church, not apart from it, in strategic collaboration to make disciples of the people whose needs are being met. Our organization has a reputable model, coaching non-profits and churches on how to work together, not only to meet specific needs of underserved children in their cities, but also in making disciples of at-risk young people through the local church. I'm certainly *for* parachurch organizations. But I understand the ramifications of what kind of spiritual devastation is looming on the horizon if this generation abandons the local church and its Christ-centered mission to make disciples.

If we are going to be followers of Jesus who change the world God's way, we must understand that abandoning the local church for a *cause* in lieu of the local church doesn't have God's bigger picture in mind. And while we, imperfect followers of Jesus, are defectively trying to get it right in our human deficiencies, the body of Christ can learn some valuable insights from the Coca-Cola Company: *think* globally but *serve* locally.

Mission Possible

When I wasn't in school, working part time for Delta Airlines, or serving my local church, I volunteered with *Mission Possible*. This was the ministry organization, founded by Preacher Woody, which helped me begin my relationship with Christ a few years back in that juvenile detention center.

Preacher Woody was the most influential spiritual leader in my life and my closest mentor. He was a redeeming father figure, renewing my view of what a father should be after suffering so much abuse and deep wounds from my biological father. He taught me countless life lessons that stand as pillars for my faith and how it's thrust into action today. One of the most crucial lessons I learned from Preacher Woody was how to be a *giver*. He is undeniably, one of the most generous people I've ever met in my life. I have never seen him go one day without sniffing out a person in need and doing a kind deed to help that person. On many occasions, I was *that* person. Preacher Woody lived by the scriptural mantra "It is more blessed to give than receive." From this man I learned how to live by faith; understanding that a life of faith is a life that constantly finds its breath in *giving* and *serving*. This kind of life is fueled by compassion for blood and mercy for oxygen.

After *Hurricane Andrew* hit South Florida in 1992, Preacher Woody and his team were among the first responders providing aid and relief to this decimated region, and perhaps more importantly, one of the organizations that kept providing aid long after the initial relief efforts had ceased. It was serving on the Mission Possible team that taught me most about putting my faith into action, training my eye to be bountiful in giving, and understanding that what we do for others is what really matters, especially when we serve those who could never repay us in this lifetime. When Jesus invites us into a cause to serve the less fortunate, he invites us into a cause larger than life.

In Luke 14, Jesus had been invited to the home of a Pharisee. The Pharisees were a people steeped in religious tradition and all too often; they allowed their tradition to stand between them and a genuine relationship with God. The Pharisees loved the praise and applause of men over God himself. They basked in the opulence of their prominent social circles. Much of their religion was put forth as showmanship, being frequently rebuked by Jesus as hypocrites. When they held parties, they only invited the elitist influential socialites who had the capabilities of returning the favor and repaying the honor. When Jesus showed up at the home of this Pharisee and observed their pomp, religious snobbery and self-serving social parading, he addressed a parable to the host of the party:

> He said also to the man who had invited him, "When you give a dinner or a banquet, do not invite your friends or your brothers or your relatives or rich neighbors, lest they also invite you in return and you be repaid. But when you give a feast, invite the poor, the crippled, the lame, the blind, and you will be blessed, because they cannot repay you. For you will be repaid at the resurrection of the just." (Luke 14:12-14)

John Wooden once said, "You can't live a perfect day without doing something for someone who will never be able to repay you." I think Jesus would agree. And Preacher Woody lived with that kind of resolve.

Through Mission Possible, I began revisiting juvenile detention centers and sharing my testimony. God reminded me that everything I had been through as a kid wasn't to be wasted. My suffering wasn't just for my redemption; it was also for the redemption of others. Countless young people needed to hear my story. Especially those incarcerated with the same despair, sense of hopelessness, and bleakness I shouldered when I was locked up. I always shared my story in the context of His-story, pointing to Jesus as the author and finisher of my life transformation. I wanted the youth in jails to understand that the key to finding your dance with destiny isn't found in sheer positive thinking or human strength of will, and it's not just in turning over a new religious leaf; this truly *new* life was afforded through a spirit-empowered relationship with Jesus.

Preacher Woody also taught me that where God's finger points, his hand will provide. I went on countless missionary trips with this faith-filled man of God. There were times we left for a journey not having enough money to return home, but every single time God provided in an awe-inspiring, unimaginable fashion. I saw God providing through the simple childlike faith of an aged man who was convinced that if God said it, we don't have to sweat it. This stout confidence was huge for me as a young follower of Christ. I discovered early on that if we put God's kingdom first in all of our affairs, we would never have to sweat where our next meal or provisions will come from.

When I was 22-years-old, I was invited to preach a youth revival in a little town in West Virginia. It was the middle of the summer and I lived in scorching South Florida. The tires on my car were so bald I could see a shiny reflection of my face in the rubber. I had a full tank of fuel and about $40 to my name. This would be just enough to get me to WV if I kept the air condition off in the car and preserved fuel. I had a hundred and one reasons for not going, but I sensed deeply that God wanted me to take this trip. I set out on the journey and for the first 180 miles or so, I was rationalizing the need to turn around and go back home. "My tires won't make it," I reasoned. I was sweating up a river with the AC turned off. As I drove northbound on I-95 up Florida's coast, I looked at my arm hanging out the window and joked with God, "I'm so poor, I don't even have a watch to tell what time it is." I chuckled and sensed God smiling upon my humor as I continued this journey alone.

I made it to WV some fourteen-hours later. The town was so far back in the woods they had to pipe in artificial sunlight. Well, not really, but I don't think they got their Sunday newspapers until Tuesday. But it was in this little country town that I met some of the most down-to-earth, hard-working, honest, and generous people on the planet. We held revival meetings for five straight days in a little country church. The second day of the revival, a mechanic in the church realized the baldness of my tires on the car. He took my car and gave me another car to borrow for the week. At the end of the week, he brought it back with brand new tires on it, professionally detailed and waxed, and the engine purring like a kitten after a much needed tune up. I was in awe. Then the church gave me a very generous love offering which exceeded above and beyond my travel expenses. And here's the real kicker: the pastor handed me a little plush box. "I think you need one of these," he said. I opened it up and it was a shiny new watch. Someone had put it in the offering plate, noticing the young preacher didn't have a means to tell time. I think it was a subtle hint I may have been preaching too long! But it was much more than that. Remember my little joke with God as I was driving up the interstate? I know God was the one cracking jokes and smiling now, but more significantly, my heavenly Father was teaching me a timeless principle that I must never forget:

> "But seek first the kingdom of God and his righteousness, and all these things will be added to you." (Matthew 6:33 ESV)

God wanted me to know something that would be the underpinning of my ministry for decades to come: put my kingdom first, and you and your family will never lack. It's that simple. Take care of God's business and He will take care of yours. That trip to WV taught me valuable lessons about God's faithfulness at the onset of my ministry, but the real winners in that whole deal was the forty-plus teenagers who gave their lives to Christ during those revival meetings. I recently received an email from a parent of one of those youth, now grown up and serving the Lord on the mission field.

At the end of the day, our faithfulness in serving Jesus is not just about us; it's about finding our dance with destiny, impacting people's lives, and being a part of shaping eternity. God invites us into this dance. We can be like the people in Luke 14:16-24 who made lame excuses about why they couldn't join the host (God) at his dinner party, or we can lay aside our reserves and come wholeheartedly alongside God in His quest to change the world (1 Corinthians 3:9). When we throw ourselves unreservedly into God's service, not only is the *mission possible*, victory is inevitable. We cannot lose in this lifetime when we seek first his kingdom in all our affairs.

I believe God reserves His greatest rewards and blessings for those who spend their lives on serving people who could never in this lifetime repay them. With that said, who are you serving? If your trying to decipher God's will for your life, that may be the first clue to discovering your divine dance with destiny. Find a Christ-centered cause, and begin serving someone else.

Chapter Nine
The Least of These

Some wish to live within the sound of a chapel bell; I wish to run a rescue mission within a yard of hell. ~ C.T. Studd

Truly, I say to you, as you did it to one of the least of these my brothers, you did it to me. ~ Jesus (Matthew 25:40)

Jesus… associated with the outcasts; he spoke with them, touched them, ate with them, loved them. ~ John Ortberg

Her beauty on ice was captivating…

Our church college group went ice-skating one night in early December. I couldn't skate very well, on ice that is, so much of my evening was passed entertaining little children in the center of the rink. Yet I was constantly distracted, or enchanted rather, by the girl in the fleecy white sweater skating gracefully around the perimeter of my kiddy circle. Cindy was the new girl in our college group. And she was drop dead gorgeous! But more than that, she had a mysterious aura about her that spoke of a deeper beauty than what meets the eye. At the end of the evening one of my friends introduced me to Cindy. I tried to play it cool like it was just another casual introduction; but truthfully, my heart was pounding on the inside.

Over the next few weeks, whenever I was invited to one of our college group gatherings, my first thought was, "Will Cindy be there?" After several group outings to movies, volleyball games, and other social get-togethers, I finally mustered the courage to ask

Cindy out on a date. We went to a restaurant called R.J. Gators, indulged in Cajun-style chicken wings, played trivia via the overhead screens, and had some of the most meaningful conversation I had in a long time. I sensed I wasn't just sitting across the table from a girl with a dazzling smile, I was engaging in deep conversation with a person whom I really felt got my heart. She seemed to understand its beating and rhythm.

Cindy had a wonderful sense of humor. She could laugh at petty things that were irritating to me. Sometimes that irritated me even more but graced me with a sense of security at the same time. Being around her, I learned that some things in life didn't need to be taken so seriously. I also loved that she had a very simple outlook on life. Money, material things, or lofty ambitions didn't move her. She modestly took life one day at a time without getting too emotional over the highs or the lows. Her strength was anchored in a worldview that God had everything under control, good and bad, and He could be trusted no matter what.

What I found in Cindy was more than a romantic affection; I had found a best friend. It's been said, "A friend is someone who knows the song in your heart and can sing it back to you when you have forgotten the words." Nothing could describe our relationship more perfectly. Cindy got my passion. She understood the song in my heart. And she could sing it back to me whenever I forgot the words. We were polar opposites in personality, and yet that is what made us *complete*. Regarding marriage, the Bible says the two shall become one, not one shall depict the two. Her strengths compensated for my weaknesses and vice versa.

Cindy and I were married in November of 1996 at Northwood Baptist Church in West Palm Beach, Florida. Her parents gave us a phenomenal wedding and then we were off to spend our honeymoon in Hilton Head, South Carolina. The first morning of our honeymoon, Cindy drove our vehicle into a concrete pole at the fuel station. It smashed in the door of the driver's side. Characteristic of her, she laughed, already fathoming a story worth telling the grandchildren. Characteristic of me, I overreacted, calculating the increase in our now mutual insurance note and the instant decrease in trade-in value with the vehicle. Either way, we both laugh at it now and tell the story with a smile. This was just the beginning of God teaching me I could learn a great deal from Cindy's whimsical approach to life. Some things just don't need to be taken so seriously.

Love much. Laugh often. Live well.

That was Cindy's approach to life. I had a hard time understanding that philosophy early on in our marriage. But I'm thankful today that I understand the essential roles that loving much and laughing often play into living well. God gave me a beautiful gift in Cindy, and she helped me to learn these life-changing values.

Breakaway Beginnings

Shortly after Cindy and I were married, we began a small Bible study in a nearby juvenile facility. It was a S.T.O.P. Camp very similar to the one I was in as a teenager. This camp was for low-risk juvenile offenders to rehabilitate, go to school, and work in a wilderness environment. We began coming in on Saturday nights, giving the youths snacks, showing Gospel films, and facilitating Bible study discussions. Cindy's home baked cookies were the main draw!

Preacher Woody had given me a 16mm film projector and a few Christian films. Even at this time, the 16mm format was somewhat outdated, but we used what we had. The Bible says if we are faithful in a few things, God will entrust us with more. At first, we only had four youths show up. But we learned quickly that when you are building a ministry targeting kids who have struggled with abandonment issues all their lives, consistency and commitment are the prerequisites to building trust. They aren't interested in hit-and-run preachers who sermonize with their Bibles and then fade off into the sunset, never to be seen again. They want to know that the people talking most about God are the same people who are going to be sticking around long after others have bailed out on them.

One of the greatest needs of delinquents is to discover a sense of security and trust in those representing, or re-presenting, the Gospel; that these storytellers of Jesus are here for the long haul to help them navigate through the challenging issues of adolescence and recovery, and not just preaching a couple of sermons and moving on. Once they know you are committed to an enduring relationship, they are comfortable asking the tough questions about faith and spirituality. Until you have earned that trust and respect by investing in their emotional security, you will always be seen in the same framework of those who have abandoned them, regardless of how good your intentions may be, or how amazingly true is your Gospel. That's where commitment and consistency play a major role in ministering to kids with issues of abandonment.

Commitment and consistency are the stocks and bonds we must faithfully invest to build trust in young people's lives. Once the juveniles saw that we consistently showed up on Saturday nights even if only one or two youths attended our Bible study, others began buying into our stock. Trust was fostered and more kids began showing up for Bible study. I don't think it hurt that Cindy baked them scrumptious cookies every week, too! I love to tell people that *Breakaway Outreach* began with one small batch of homemade cookies and it was *Game On* from there! We simply gave God the little we had and he multiplied it exceedingly. Eventually, every youth in the facility began voluntarily attending our program on Saturday nights. God started doing amazing things in the lives of these teenagers simply because we began demonstrating Jesus' love through a few small things (cookies and 16mm films).

Cindy and I loved stopping for frozen yogurt after every Saturday night service, a convenient amenity on our route home. We loved to talk about all the wonderful things God was doing in this ministry over a smooth and refreshing cup of frozen yogurt. These were great times in our small beginnings.

After building consistency with our Bible studies, we began organizing what we called "Super Saturday" events. We brought in basketball teams to play ball with the camp residents, did team-based "Wacky Olympic" relay races, and other interactive recreational activities with the youths; all followed by a clear presentation of the Gospel. The youths were having a blast learning about God. Their positive attitudes carried over into the rest of the week, and morale in the camp was at an all-time high as juvenile justice administrators were left scratching their heads at the success of our program. Word soon spread to other juvenile facilities throughout the region. It wasn't long before we were inundated with invitations from other juvie institutions that were desperate for programs that *worked* with kids, and they didn't care that it was faith-based, as long as it made some kind of positive difference in their lives.

This movement would later give birth to what is known today as *Breakaway Outreach*; a non-profit organization turning the tide of delinquency and poverty one child at a time by reaching at-risk youth and under-served communities through urban outreach, after school programs in low-income neighborhoods, juvenile justice intervention, summer camps for prisoners' children, mentoring relationships, and community-wide initiatives.

Ricky's Story

Ricky was one of many boys at the Stop Camp whose life was changed by the power of the Gospel. Every Saturday night as we concluded our Bible study, and while we were packing up our belongings, this fourteen-year-old lad was already on the phone with his mother reiterating everything he learned about God that night. Back home, he had a twelve-year-old brother named Reuben, who spent a lot of time eavesdropping in on those telephone conversations. He knew there was something different about Ricky, and he would soon get a closer peek at what was going on in his brother's life.

After Ricky was released from the camp, we stayed in touch with him and continued to encourage him with books, study helps, and discipleship materials. We went to his home in Vero Beach and met his mother and younger brother, Reuben. We visited often and took them to youth group meetings, concerts, and the beach. One night we took Ricky and Reuben out for dinner and a baseball game. Coming from a single parent, low-income family, they didn't get many opportunities to eat out. So even our trip to McDonald's faired to them the elegance of a five star restaurant. After some cheeseburgers, fries, and milkshakes, we headed out to a minor league baseball game. That evening, Reuben seemed captivated by our kindness. Even though he didn't articulate it vocally, his visage seemed to question: "Why would these people take time out of their lives to drive all the way up from West Palm Beach, take us to fun and exciting places, and pay our way?" Somewhere around the 5th inning of the baseball game, Reuben and I sat comfortably with our feet dangling over the empty bleacher seats in front of us and engaged in a discussion that answered some of these questions.

By the end of the game, Reuben seemed to have a lucid take on our motivation. It was all about the kindness of our Savior, whose love compels us to love and serve others with the same measure of kindness that has been lavished on us. Reuben had also come to understand more vividly the Gospel story that had changed his brother's life. That evening after the baseball game, in the backseat of our truck, Reuben prayed and invited Jesus Christ to become the Lord of his life. Over the next few years we witnessed God at work in their lives doing wonderful things. Ricky made good on a goal to become the first person in his family to ever attend college; and the story of these two boys served as an inspiration for our ministry in later developing programs that reach out to younger siblings of juvenile offenders and children of prisoners.

Youth Gone Wild

As we continued to provide services in juvenile centers, youth inmates would often ask us if we had any programs for their younger siblings. "I don't want my younger brother or sister to end up where I am," they would say. This prompted us to devise strategies in ministering to families of incarcerated teens, and specifically younger children, who were six times more likely to end up in jail simply because they had a parent or older sibling already there.

Before we had any structured programs in place, we invited several former juvenile offenders and their younger siblings on a youth outing to Orlando where *Universal Studios* was hosting a youth event featuring Christian bands and speakers. They called this *Rock the Universe!* Our kids were pumped. A friend of ours rented two 15-passenger vans for us to take the kids to Orlando and attend the weekend event. We also had some ministry partners sponsor the kids to stay at a hotel. We had more rooms than chaperones, so we had to trust a few teenagers unsupervised at night with their own rooms (a policy we quickly corrected after this trip). We had a very well behaved group but I still felt a little dicey having some in a room alone. At any rate, the kids had a blast riding roller coasters, eating popcorn, *jamming out* to bands, and hearing life-changing messages from some key youth communicators.

Everything seemed to be okay until the morning of checkout.

The hotel clerk handed me the bill. My heart seemed to stop beating for a second or two and then proceeded to play ping-pong with my throat and my stomach. I couldn't believe my eyes. It was over $900 for two nights! Room service, video games, and dirty movies had all been charged to Room #252. My adrenaline was like fire in my blood. I approached the van determined to find out who was in Room #252, still shell-shocked about what to do once I did find out who was responsible. Praying feverishly under my breath, I opened the van door and authoritatively asked, "Who was in Room 252?"

Nobody answered.

"Who was in room number 252?" I repeated.

There was dead silence.

After a momentary hush, which felt more like an hour, a youth in the back of the van spoke up and said, "We didn't have Room 252. That wasn't part of our group."

I paused momentarily, and looked back down at the invoice. The name across the top of the bill was addressed to a church in central Florida. The clerk had mistakenly given us their invoice. I immediately rushed back into the hotel and traded it in for our *flawless* invoice, and paid that thing faster than a NASCAR pit stop. How do you spell R E L I E F? I'll tell you how I spell "relief," it's the name of that youth pastor printed at the top of that $900 bill! I wouldn't have wanted to be in his shoes – or those kids' shoes – when they got back to church on Sunday.

Our kids had behaved immaculately all weekend, and they had much to talk about on the way home. Once they got beyond the humor of that church's *Youth Group Gone Wild* escapade, they zeroed in on all the fun they had in the name of Jesus. Most of these children had never even been to a theme park before, and we gave them a childhood experience they would never forget.

That initial trip to Orlando inspired our *KidVenturez* program, which now provides spiritual retreats, weekend adventures, recreational outings, and field trips for hundreds of disadvantaged kids every year.

Denny's Story

Not every story from those early beginnings turned out favorably. One resident left Stop Camp and was killed in a drive-by shooting a week later. Others re-offended and went on to become what inmates refer to as "lifers." A *lifer* is basically someone who is serving a self-imposed sentence behind bars because the benefits in the system outweigh the hellish conditions on the streets. We've witnessed many good-hearted kids deliberately get into trouble and become repeat offenders purely because the conditions in the juvenile center were safer and more secure than life on the streets, the instability of their homes, or the violence in their hood. Their fear drives them to re-offend, because getting caught is suitably a reprieve for them. Oftentimes the structure of the rehabilitative system gives them more of a familial environment than what they've ever had at home.

Denny was a youth who lived in our neighborhood, just the next street over from our apartment. We met him when he was twelve-years-old and I initiated a mentoring relationship with him at that time. His mother was a crack addict who suffered from post-traumatic stress disorder in connection with an earlier robbery at her workplace. Living in a dysfunctional home without any rules or boundaries caused Denny to live out of deep-rooted insecurities.

Every opportunity we had, we took Denny and his neighborhood friend, Troy, on special outings. They went with us to church, youth groups, and even to some of our juvenile center services. Their favorite outing was when we took them for ice cream, and not just for the sugar rush; they genuinely seemed to savor the meaningful conversations we shared about God, faith, and life, all over a rich double dip cone of chocolate with sprinkles on top.

In 1999, *Breakaway Outreach* provided scholarships for Denny and Troy to attend summer camp in Panama City with a local youth group. The group consisted of about forty teens from the West Palm Beach area, but once we arrived in Panama City we would be joining a much larger youth group of about two hundred students from a church in Central Florida. It may have been the same group that rang up the $900 hotel bill at Universal Studios a year before! I'm not sure. But the Central Florida church was hosting the summer camp and we must play by their rules. They had mailed us a copy of the rules and guidelines of what to bring, and not to bring, prior to leaving South Florida. We made sure Denny and Troy were familiar with the rules and contraband items, this being the very first Christian summer camp they ever attended.

When we arrived in Panama City, we were blown away with the mischievousness we saw in the group from Central Florida. They began unpacking their travel bags, unveiling all kinds of paraphernalia that was on the *"Things NOT to Bring to Camp"* list we received before leaving home. They pulled out *panzerchecks*, Tiger tanks, bazookas, and smoke grenades… well not exactly, but they did have an overabundance of water balloons and other illegal imports for pranks, which had been strictly forbidden. I saw it on Denny's face, "So this is what *Christian* camp is all about!"

I could smell trouble brewing… and prank strategies formulating.

During the worship service of the opening night, I was appalled. As the worship leader attempted to sing songs, this group from Central Florida, numbering around two hundred students, simply carried on obliviously in social conversations as if the guy on stage didn't even exist. Worship was the farthest thing from their agenda. It was one of the most blatantly disrespectful atmospheres I have ever witnessed in any youth ministry environment. This complete spiritual disdain, or social circus if you will, was finally abruptly interrupted when the worship leader himself, utterly annoyed, yelled into the microphone, "Would you all please SHUT UP?!"

I sensed the worship leader had never faced this kind of environment before. He was agitated and they had gotten under his skin. *I wanted to invite him to a juvenile center where it seemed he would get more respect.* I couldn't blame him for losing his cool. It was sheer chaos. I feared mostly for Denny and Troy, that they wouldn't be able to truly capture a meaningful spiritual experience in this parade of insolence. But God has his ways of changing the game... quickly!

After that evening worship service, the youths went back to their cabins. It didn't take long for me to get a call about Denny and Troy. I was summoned to the "principle's office" to deal with "my" kids. Apparently, their had been some words exchanged between Denny and another camper, and Denny had shoved the boy. Knowing that Denny had been sent to camp on scholarship and that he was on juvenile justice probation already, the mother of the boy demanded that Denny leave camp. Denny took full responsibility for his behavior, but was ostracized more because of his label as a delinquent than for his squabble with the other camper.

There was no grace, no reconciliatory ministry, no love, no mercy. They wanted Denny and Troy off the premises.

It was Monday night, and we didn't have a vehicle to drive home in because we rode with the church bus to camp. But the Central Florida youth pastor was forcing us to take our kids out of camp so we had no other options but to rent a hotel room at our own expense, stay there until the end of the week, and hitch a ride back home on the church bus with the South Florida group on Friday. My wife and I were determined to see this as an opportunity, not a disappointment. We rented a hotel room and spent the rest of the week with our boys as if this were their camping experience. We swam in the pool, had Bible studies, played games, and engaged in life-changing discussions with Denny and Troy. We turned that Panama City hotel into a makeshift summer camp facility and as a result, two souls were saved. At the end of the week, both Denny and Troy prayed to receive Christ, and both wanted to be baptized. We baptized them right there in the pool as guests of the hotel applauded in celebration. We knew this was a *Romans 8:28* moment; God had brought everything together for His good.

But this whole incident could've turned for bad… *really bad.* Denny and Troy could've left camp feeling like outcasts, pushed further away from Jesus due to the nature of what happened that first night at camp, if we hadn't intervened and demonstrated God's restorative love to them. I can't imagine what might've happened if they had left camp rejected by God's people and had no one to shepherd their nomadic souls.

Coincidentally, all of this happened just a couple of months after the *Columbine High School massacre,* where Eric Harris and Dylan Klebold killed twelve students and one teacher while injuring twenty-one other students. Denny and Troy's story had many parallels to Eric and Dylan's story from a social standpoint, and the Columbine culprits had also been to a Christian youth event in which they were barred just a few weeks before the shooting. We will never understand all the correlations involved in cases when kids turn violent, but one thing is certain: labeling troubled youth and shoving them aside will NOT solve our societal problems or serve Jesus well in our generation. We must advocate for unlovable kids even when they don't deserve it. If we don't *break* into their lives with the love of Christ, they will without doubt *break* into our lives through aberrant rampages like Eric Harris and Dylan Klebold. In the end, society always loses when the church ousts troubled kids.

Shortly after returning home from camp, I wrote that Central Florida youth pastor one of my "Apostle Paul" letters, you know, the ones where you get to tell someone off by *speaking the truth in love*. I referred to the Columbine incident and the parallels with Denny and Troy's backgrounds, and then made the point that I was glad that Denny and Troy lived in our neighborhood and not his.

Was I a little too harsh in my rebuke? I wondered.

I admit that I struggled with that tension for several years until I received a phone call in February 2006 to come and preside over Denny's funeral. He had been killed in a robbery at his own residence just before his 21st birthday, due to a ripple effect from his mother's drug habits. There was an indescribable peace in my heart at Denny's funeral. I knew that he was in heaven, and the Holy Spirit assured our hearts of this. But the real settlement in my soul was this: when eternity is hanging in the balance, we don't have time to *not* speak the truth in love. We don't have time to *not* advocate for the outcast. What if we hadn't defended Denny's self-worth that week in Panama despite his initial behavior? What if we hadn't taken money out of our own pockets to give Denny and Troy that redemptive camping experience at the hotel? What if we just expelled them from our programs like the youth pastor from Central Florida did? There were so many "What ifs?" The story could've ended much worse. Denny's soul could've been lost forever. But even though his life on earth was tragically snuffed out early, we knew that Denny had responded to God's grace and taken the right steps in faith because someone had stuck their necks out for him, even when his actions didn't merit it. There is a way to love the sinner while *not* condoning the sin. We did that with Denny.

There were over four hundred young people who attended Denny's funeral. After I shared his testimony and presented a clear explanation of the Gospel, over fifty teenagers responded to my invitation to receive Christ. I sensed Jesus smiling and Denny dancing in the portals of heaven.

Life is too short and eternity is too long for you and I to presume that we get to choose who is worthy of grace. The truth is, none of us are worthy.

It's only because of the grace of our Lord Jesus Christ that we find acceptance with God; nothing more, and nothing less (Ephesians 2:8-9). We should view every person in the light of His grace, not picking and choosing who should be allowed into our religious circles based on our tolerance criterion. I have chosen over the years to err on the side of grace. It seems to be the only thing that truly *wins* over all human messiness in this lifetime and the one to come.

In 2007, we launched our own summer camp experience in North Carolina for prisoners' children, inner city kids, and other at-risk youth. Every year we see kids' lives changed through this camping adventure. Many of these children wouldn't be accepted at some mainstream church camps, but that's exactly why we started this camp. So kids can come and have a chance to hear and respond to the Gospel story without being branded by their past or present social labels. Every year, I love to go to the top of the mountain overlooking the campgrounds. Every year, I thank God for the amazing things He is doing in the lives of each and every one of these unique kids…

… and every year, I think of Denny.

A Runaway Slave and a Starfish

Around A.D. 61, the Apostle Paul wrote a letter to a Christian brother named Philemon who was a leader in the Colossian church. This New Testament epistle is often an overlooked book in the Bible, dealing with forgiveness and redemption for a troubled youth. Paul, who is in prison (probably in either Rome or Ephesus), writes this letter of advocacy in defense of a troubled young person named Onesimus. Onesimus was probably in his late teens when Paul wrote this letter. Onesimus was a former slave of Philemon and apparently had stolen from him, took flight as a fugitive, and was later captured and placed in the same prison as Paul. It was here that Paul presumably leads this young man to saving faith in Jesus, then has the boldness to write Philemon and urge him to take Onesimus back, no longer as a slave, but as a dear brother in Christ, removing all the labels from his past status as slave and purging his criminal offenses.

This was an unbelievably risky stance taken by Paul and perhaps an even greater risk for Philemon. Around this same time, all of Rome was shocked when a prefect of the city, Pedanius Secundus, was murdered by one of his slaves. Consequently, Roman senate enforced a law already on books and put to death 400 of the murderer's fellow slaves – men, women, and children, even though they were innocent.[ix] This was no time to be advocating for runaway, criminal slaves. Paul did it anyway and risked his own reputation on a thief. He asked Philemon to drop all charges, asked that he be free from slave status, and esteemed as a brother in the faith. This request was unheard of in first-century Rome. What if Onesimus re-offended? Was a runaway slave worth the risk?

Did Paul's risk pay off? Whatever became of Onesimus? The Bible doesn't say. But Ignatius, Bishop of Antioch, wrote a letter some fifty years later about a man who seems to fit the description of this runaway slave. Ignatius referred to him as Onesimus, Bishop of Ephesus![x] It sounds as if Philemon regarded the instruction of Paul and took a risk himself. What happened was even more unlikely than a slave becoming a citizen, apparently that slave went on to lead the church in all of Ephesus.

One day an old man was walking along the beach. It was low tide, and the sand was littered with thousands of stranded starfish that the water had carried in and then left behind. The man began walking very carefully so as not to step on any of the beautiful creatures. Since the animals still seemed to be alive, he considered picking some of them up and putting them back in the water, where they could resume their lives. The man knew the starfish would die if left on the beach's dry sand but he reasoned that he could not possibly help them all, so he chose to do nothing and continued walking.

Soon afterward, the man came upon a small child on the beach who was feverishly throwing one starfish after another back into the sea. The old man stopped and asked the child, "What are you doing?"

"I'm saving the starfish," the child replied.

"Why waste your time? There are so many you can't save them all so what does is matter?" argued the man.

Without hesitation, the child picked up another starfish and tossed the starfish back into the water... "It matters to this one," the child explained.

That story has always stuck with me since the first time I heard it years ago. We even branded a starfish into our *Breakaway Outreach* logo to always remind us that what we do matters and that the grace of our Lord Jesus Christ is all-sufficient for the *least* of these. We understand that every child matters to God, whether fatherless, impoverished, incarcerated, delinquent, underprivileged, or abandoned. And while much of society may marginalize these children, overlook them, or even write them off as hopeless due to their risk factors, we believe that every young person has redemptive purpose through Jesus Christ.

I was that *starfish* at one time. Someone picked me up and gave me hope. Ricky was a starfish. Denny was a starfish. Paul was a starfish. Onesimus was a starfish. And yet, each one of them found hope in the life-giving message of the Gospel. Perhaps some of the greatest giants we will ever overcome in our lifetime will involve standing up for the outcast, voicing a defense for the fatherless, restoring justice in our cities, bringing good news to the imprisoned, reaching out to the impoverished, advocating for the destitute, and rescuing the abused, abandoned, and forsaken.

Our dance with destiny will never be complete without crying out for those who can't cry out for themselves. For, their giants... are our giants.

Chapter Ten
I Hope You Dance

People living deeply have no fear of death. ~ Anaïs Nin

Fear is a darkroom where negatives develop. ~ Usman B. Asif

It is the LORD who goes before you. He will be with you; he will not leave you or forsake you. Do not fear or be dismayed. ~ Moses (Deuteronomy 31:8 ESV)

I can picture young Joshua sitting around a warm campfire with Moses one evening, leaning in intensely as the firewood popped, keenly absorbing every last word of encouragement he could glean from his aging predecessor. Moses' days were numbered and Joshua's name was being summoned. Joshua soaked up Moses' wisdom like a sponge. He revered his mentor with admirable respect, maybe even feeling a bit sorry for Moses' failure to enter the Promised Land himself. What final words of instruction or grand lesson on leadership will Moses choose to leave with Joshua in his final exhortation?

"Do not fear."

And in his final hours, Moses would summon all of Israel together to hear the unflinching promises of God:

> So Moses continued to speak these words to all Israel. And he said to them, "I am 120 years old today. I am no longer able to go out and come in. The LORD has said to me, 'You shall not go over this Jordan.' The LORD your God himself will go over before you. He

will destroy these nations before you, so that you shall dispossess them, and Joshua will go over at your head, as the LORD has spoken. And the LORD will do to them as he did to Sihon and Og, the kings of the Amorites, and to their land, when he destroyed them. And the LORD will give them over to you, and you shall do to them according to the whole commandment that I have commanded you. Be strong and courageous. Do not fear or be in dread of them, for it is the LORD your God who goes with you. He will not leave you or forsake you." Then Moses summoned Joshua and said to him in the sight of all Israel, "Be strong and courageous, for you shall go with this people into the land that the LORD has sworn to their fathers to give them, and you shall put them in possession of it. It is the LORD who goes before you. He will be with you; he will not leave you or forsake you. Do not fear or be dismayed."
(Deuteronomy 31:1-8 ESV)

It was Joshua's time to step up and begin his *dance with destiny*. He must learn from the previous generation who failed to follow God wholeheartedly into the Promised Land, not to make the same mistakes. Why did they fail?

Fear.

Their hearts melted when they looked at the size of the giants in the land they must dispossess. They wanted the real estate, but they didn't want to fight for it… they wanted the glory but they had no guts. Moses had sent out twelve spies to go into the land and bring back a strategy for battle. But instead of returning with a *good* report, they brought back a *fearful* report:

At the end of forty days they returned from spying out the land. And they came to Moses and Aaron and to all the congregation of the people of Israel in the wilderness of Paran, at Kadesh. They brought back word to them and to all the congregation, and showed them the fruit of the land. And they told him, "We came to the land to which you sent us. It flows with milk and honey, and this is its fruit. However, the people who dwell in the land are strong, and the cities are fortified and very large. And besides, we saw the descendants of Anak there. The Amalekites dwell in the land of the Negeb. The Hittites, the Jebusites, and the Amorites dwell in the hill country. And the Canaanites dwell by the sea, and along the Jordan." But Caleb quieted the people before Moses and said, "Let us go up at once and occupy it, for we are well able to overcome it." Then the men who had gone up with him said, "We are not able to go up against the people, for they are stronger than we are." So they brought to the people of Israel a bad report of the land that they had spied out, saying, "The land, through which we have gone to spy it out, is a land that devours its inhabitants, and all the people that we saw in it are of great height. And there we saw the Nephilim (the sons of Anak, who come from the Nephilim), and we seemed to ourselves like grasshoppers, and so we seemed to them." (Numbers 13:25-33 ESV)

Only two of the twelve spies Moses sent actually returned with a determined spirit of faith and resolve; Joshua and Caleb. The other ten (the majority) had doomed an entire generation. Their fear was contagious and crippling. It spread like wildfire. The hearts of the people melted. Instead of going on the offensive and following God wholly into the unknown, they began living in a defensive posture, even forming their own coup to lead the people back into Egyptian bondage.

Then all the congregation raised a loud cry, and the people wept that night. And all the people of Israel grumbled against Moses and Aaron. The whole congregation said to them, "Would that we had died in the land of Egypt! Or would that we had died in this wilderness! Why is the LORD bringing us into this land, to fall by the sword? Our wives and our little ones will become a prey. Would it not be better for us to go back to Egypt?" And they said to one another, "Let us choose a leader and go back to Egypt." (Numbers 14:1-4 ESV)

Fearfulness always causes us to choose leadership that will coddle our fears and anesthetize us in our unfaithfulness to God. So Israel rebelled against the godly leadership of Moses and formed their own leadership to turn their hearts away from such a bold venture. Consequently, God had to wait forty years for an entire generation to die off in the wilderness so that he could replace it with a younger generation that would take him at his word and storm the hills of the Promised Land, slay the giants, possess the territory, and finally give God the *glory* he waited forty years for. In the end, fear always robs God of his glory because it causes us to fail to go where God has already gone before us to orchestrate victory.

In Joshua 2, we see that Moses' successor learned from those failures that it's better to send only two spies full of faith, vision, and courage into the land, as opposed to twelve who would return full of doubt, trepidation, skepticism, and contagious fear. He was now being called by God to step up and lead the next generation into the land God had sworn to the previous generation, and the paramount leadership quality he must possess is *courage*. God had already constructed *13-foot coffins* for every one of those giants in Canaan. But it took forty years until a people emerged who would have the courage to dance with destiny, slay those giants, and bury those coffins.

We must understand that faith isn't the absence of fear; it's the antidote to fear. Courage isn't the absence of fear; it's the mastery of it. Living fearlessly doesn't mean we will never be afraid, it simply means we will not succumb to our fears. We will face them, master them, and overrun them through the power of the Holy Spirit who gives us supernatural courage to face insurmountable odds.

Was Joshua afraid? *You betcha!* He was human like us. Look what God commands him:

> No man shall be able to stand before you all the days of your life. Just as I was with Moses, so I will be with you. I will not leave you or forsake you. Be strong and courageous, for you shall cause this people to inherit the land that I swore to their fathers to give them. Only be strong and very courageous, being careful to do according to all the law that Moses my servant commanded you. Do not turn from it to the right hand or to the left, that you may have good success wherever you go. This Book of the Law shall not depart from your mouth, but you shall meditate on it day and night, so that you may be careful to do according to all that is written in it. For then you will make your way prosperous, and then you will have good success. Have I not commanded you? Be strong and courageous. Do not be frightened, and do not be dismayed, for the LORD your God is with you wherever you go." (Joshua 1:5-9 ESV)

God tells his young leader over and over again throughout the book of Joshua, "Be strong and courageous; do not be afraid." If Joshua didn't struggle with fear, God would've never needed to command him to be bold and courageous. The beauty of Joshua and Caleb's spirit is that they weren't driven by their fears. They were driven despite their fears! As Eleanor Roosevelt rightly observed, "You gain strength, courage, and confidence by every experience in which you really stop to look fear in the face. You must do the thing which you think you cannot do."

This was Joshua's strength and Caleb's resolve. They never let fear master them. They didn't focus on the size of their giants; they focused on the size of their God. That enabled them to live fearlessly and face their giants.

Getting Out of The Boat

My four-year-old, Mackenzie, is a warrior princess who loves beauty, fairy tales, and anything with a sense of adventure. And she gives me a ton of sermon illustrations. One day she swaggered up to my wife sanguinely and said, "Mommy, I want to invite Jesus to come into my heart." Her mother couldn't have been more proud. Then a few seconds later she concluded, "I want to invite Cinderella into my heart too!"

Kenzie loves to watch sharks on *Animal Planet* and *Discovery Channel*. I asked her if she wanted to go swimming with the sharks one day and she said, "Yes, only if you come too."

Looks like my little girl will never swim with the sharks!

For a compromise, we went swimming with manatees in Florida when some friends took our family out on a V.I.P. private tour along the Homosassa River. We boated out to a site swarming with manatees, finding ourselves instantly surrounded by these huge creatures drifting all around the boat. Our friend, a professional manatee guide, jumped right in and started snorkeling with them. I quickly followed, taking Mackenzie and my son, Zachary, along with me. I expected Stephanie, my oldest daughter to dive right in behind me… it didn't happen. She stood paralyzed in fear on the deck above.

Stephanie is typically the daredevil in our family. She gets that from her Momma. So I was somewhat taken aback to see her afraid of this experience. In this moment she was stuck. I hadn't seen her this fearful in a long time.

I gently urged Steph to get in but she wouldn't budge, and I didn't want to pressure her so I took Zachary and Mackenzie over to pet the manatees. A few minutes later Steph was in tears. I knew her dilemma. She didn't want to miss this experience but she was terrified to get in the water, debilitated by the size of the manatees.

To add to her regret, our guide had an underwater camera, capturing video and pictures of this epic adventure. Steph's fear told her to play it safe here, and she was struggling somewhere between fishing for courage and heeding those voices. The water was too intimidating in itself, let alone the teeming of these huge marine mammals also known as "Sea Cows."

In what would come to be a defining moment, I made my daughter this solemn promise: "Honey, I can't promise you that in life it will always be *safe* to jump into the *waters*, but I can promise you this; If you don't jump, you will be watching this video later and you will regret not being in the picture."

I am convinced that at the end of our years it will be regrets of inaction that far outweigh the regrets of action in our lives. In other words, we will be more regretful over not being in the picture at all (playing it safe) because we were afraid to jump, rather than being in the picture, looking vulnerable, sometimes afraid, or even feeling like a failure at times.

In this moment, I can't help but to think about Peter in Matthew 14.

Imagine what it must've felt like for the seasoned-fisherman-turned-Christ-follower, clinching the frazzled ropes on the edge of the boat while His Jesus stood supernaturally on water, defiant of the threats of the storm, beckoning Peter to step out of the boat and join him in a dangerous journey into the unknown. Peter looked around cautiously. No one else was getting out of the boat. Andrew was still trying to radio the coast guard. James was more concerned with bailing water out of the boat than what was happening outside the boat. It didn't make sense to Peter. Humans aren't supposed to walk on water; especially in a raging storm. As he continues to pan his surroundings and the imminent threat of danger, he makes eye contact with Jesus. He see's a burning, sort of numbing sensation in Jesus' eyes. The closer he looks into them the more secure he feels, despite what is unfolding around him. The winds are boisterous and the violent waves jerk the boat back and forth. He glances back at the hull. John appears to be praying while others cry out in fear. Amidst the agitation of the jolts, he makes eye contact with Jesus… again. This time he locks in for good. Nothing else matters. Pleasing the heart of the one *calling* him is all that counts. It's a do-or-die, make-or-break, all-or-nothing moment. He takes that first step and all of a sudden it feels as if someone else is doing the rest. He is locked in on the eyes of Jesus – eyes that exude trust, confidence, and security, in the face of all the chaos encircling them. Peter is doing the unbelievable. He is walking on water. The other disciples begin to notice. His feat now causes inspiration to swell in the hearts of his companions. Notwithstanding the danger, they begin to sense their lives are caught up in something much *bigger* than the storm. They are on a journey with One Who is shaping eternity; a *Choreographer* whom even the winds and the waves obey!

Yes, Peter takes his eyes off Jesus momentarily, only to fall in the arms of grace. But he is unsinkable. His master *Choreographer* holds his hand. Peter need never fear getting out of the boat again. The heart of his *Choreographer* can be trusted. Peter would never have a regret at the end of his journey about not getting out of the boat. It's okay to fall sometimes, as long as we don't play it safe in the boat, clinching to our fears.

We must risk boldly for God rather than live conservatively in religious comfort. "If the highest aim of a captain were to preserve his ship, he would keep it in port forever," said Thomas Aquinas. Our goal is not to preserve our own safety, it's to learn how to trust and follow Jesus anywhere, which inevitably will take us into unknown territory. It will involve storms. It will involve waves. At times, we will sink momentarily. We will lose focus temporarily. But we must never shrink back by reducing our lives to being a mere boat-preserver.

Years ago I taped this quote by Teddy Roosevelt to the inside cover of my Bible:

> "It is not the critic who counts; not the man who points out how the strong man stumbles, or where the doer of deeds could have done them better. The credit belongs to the man who is actually in the arena, whose face is marred by dust and sweat and blood, who strives valiantly; who errs and comes short again and again; because there is not effort without error and shortcomings; but who does actually strive to do the deed; who knows the great enthusiasm, the great devotion, who spends himself in a worthy cause, who at the best knows in the end the triumph of high achievement and who at the worst, if he fails, at least he fails while daring greatly. So that his place shall never be with those cold and timid souls who know neither victory nor defeat."

What a great picture of Peter. We must always be ready to get out of the boat every time our *Choreographer* leads us. Risks will be necessary, and those afraid to take them will forfeit their dance with destiny like that first generation of Israelites who perished in the wilderness.

Once my daughter got the revelation that her regrets of inaction would hurt more than any risk taken that day, she left her fear in the boat and jumped in the water. She got a hold of the reality that if she played it "safe," she would regret it for a long time. All of a sudden danger became an adventure to live rather than a fear to avoid. Stephanie danced beautifully with the manatees that day, but more importantly, she danced with Jesus. Thucydides once said, "The bravest are surely those who have the clearest vision of what is before them, glory and danger alike, and yet notwithstanding, go out to meet it." Or as country singer Lee Ann Womack artistically reminds us, *"And when you get the choice to sit it out or dance, I hope you dance."*

I'm so glad that when my little girl was faced with the choice to sit it out or dance, she chose to dance. She lived fearlessly as she met her perceived danger with reckless abandon and ultimately swam with the giants that day. She even brought home a DVD reminiscing all of her underwater adventures that day (a video I later dubbed to the song *I Hope You Dance*). I'm thrilled that all of my children are in the video we brought back from Florida. They didn't miss the dance. Now every time my kids watch that video, they hear that song and are reminded that throughout life we will always be faced with decisions to either play it safe, or dance with Jesus into the dangerous unknown.

Moses, when faced with the fear of playing it safe, instead chose to dance by confronting Pharaoh to free his people from slavery. I'm so glad that David, instead of playing it safe with the sheep, decided to dance with destiny by challenging Goliath and the Philistines, and justice was secured for his people. Peter didn't cower in the boat; he danced with Jesus on the water and became the first leader of the church. And what about Esther? She had everything to lose by approaching the king uninvited, but she didn't play it safe when destiny was on the line. She danced – and her advocacy rescued an entire generation! God says to Nehemiah, "The walls of the city are in rubble and there's decay everywhere. Gangs are rampant. Drug dealers own the neighborhoods. Violence is abroad. I know you can play it safe here in the king's palace sippin' on Chiante and watching *King of Queens* reruns every night, but I'm inviting you into a dangerous journey to rebuild a city's dignity. Do you want to dance?"

My prayer for all my children is that, when faced with the choice of playing it safe or dancing with destiny, they choose to recklessly abandon themselves to God's call on their lives. My prayer for all of our Breakaway kids is that they learn to dance with the *Master Choreographer*, Jesus. My prayer for the church in this hour, is that it doesn't hide behind lush stained-glass windows, warming padded pews, when there is a world out there more ready for Jesus than ever before. We need more *fishers of men*, not more *keepers of the aquarium*. Our generation needs the Gospel and we can't afford to play it *safe* in this hour.

Will you rise and face your giants?

Will your story be told one hundred years from now?

Your dance with destiny hangs in the balance.

Eternity hangs in the balance.

God's glory hangs in the balance.

Millions of lost souls hang in the balance.

I pray you dance.

A Childhood Dream Fulfilled

As mentioned earlier, I grew up going to baseball games at the old Memorial Stadium ballpark on 33rd Street in Baltimore. My very first childhood dream was to be a *Baltimore Oriole* when I grew up; envisioning following in the footsteps of childhood heroes Eddie Murray and Cal Ripken, Jr.

I remember being in the left field bleachers as a kid when my hero, Cal Ripken (#8), hit his first career grand slam right over my head. It was his rookie year, September 14, 1982, versus the archrival New York Yankees. I was eleven-years-old and I can still see that baseball flying over my head today, more the size of a volleyball than a baseball. Things are always bigger through the eyes of a child; I think that's partly why Jesus said that unless we had the faith of a little child, we would never see.

In preparation for his first little league season, my seven-year-old son, Zachary, recently watched all the Cal Ripken training DVDs. On draft night, he was picked by the "Orioles." What a way to begin his first season of little league adventure! I also found out they would be wearing the old school uniforms with the logos from the 80's, the decade I collected my most memorable *Oriole* experiences. What's more, he got the number *8*.

Mere coincidence? No way!

God has a witty way of letting us know He's always a part of our dreams – even when they look a little bit different when they come into fruition decades later. This season, at 40-years old, *I am an Oriole, and more significantly, I am a Dad;* sitting on the bleachers of every game, wearing my Orioles' jersey and Orioles' cap pulling for my favorite baseball hero: Zachary Larche… a.k.a. #8.

John Eldredge wrote, "We have desires in our hearts that are core to who and what we are; they are almost mythic in their meaning, waking in us something transcendent and eternal. But we can be mistaken about how those desires will be lived out. The way in which God fulfills a desire may be different from what first awakened it."

As a child I dreamed of growing up and becoming an *Oriole*. Today, I am the Dad of a little league *Oriole*. Dreams do come true, in a way often "different from what first awakened it," as Eldredge would say. And I wouldn't have wanted it to turn out any other way;

being an *Oriole Dad* of the greatest boy in the universe far exceeds being a professional ball player hitting line drives at Camden Yards for a living.

God, thank you for this dance. Thank you for a childhood dream coming true. Thank you for the gift of fatherhood. And thank you for the amazing son and daughters I get to share this dream with as we build memories for a lifetime! Thank you for an amazing wife to dance with. Thank you for the dream job you've given me, in empowering this generation of young people to overcome their fears, face their giants, and dance with the Master Choreographer, Jesus Christ. And God, thank you for 13-foot coffins in our lives: they tell of your glory, and remind us from whence grace has brought us, and to where it carries us onward!

Still Under Construction

Some time ago, while leading a seminar in Charlotte, North Carolina, we had the opportunity to visit the *Billy Graham Library* where Ruth Bell Graham is buried. Graham, wife of world-renowned evangelist Billy Graham, was laid to rest in a simple coffin made of birch plywood, modestly crafted by an inmate at a Louisiana correctional facility.

Her epitaph reads: *"End of construction. Thank you for your patience."*

Ruth Bell Graham chose the words herself years before her death. They come from a road construction sign she once commented on, saying, "What a marvelous image for the Christian life – a work under construction until we go to be with God. That's what I want as my epitaph."

It's a beautiful reminder that our journey is a continued work of grace. When it comes to patience, I am a spiritual pauper. I'm in desperate need – as a recipient and a giver. If we are to be recipients of this grace – we need to be very quick to extend it to others.

Jonathan Edwards once said, "Grace is but glory begun, and glory is but grace perfected."

In this messy *construction zone* we live in, we have only begun in our experience of grace – our day of perfection is set apart for a much later chapter in the tomes of our spiritual journey. In this present chapter, however, we need much grace – and we need to give it abundantly.

Grace always wins!

About the Author

Throughout history God has left his mark on the world through people who have had no other agenda but Jesus. Jimmy Larche considers himself a "stagehand" for Jesus and is "consumed with a relentless passion of realizing what that might look like in the 21st Century."

He is co-founder of Breakaway Outreach, a nonprofit ministry organization serving at-risk youth, underprivileged children, and under-served communities.

As an ordained minister and international Gospel communicator, Jimmy has been preaching God's word with anointing, passion, and vibrancy for over 25 years. He is a missions mobilizer, evangelist, and outreach strategist—a frequent communicator for churches, conferences, retreats, youth groups, summer camps, evangelistic events, revival services, missions groups, and banquets.

Visit www.jimmylarche.com for more info.

For booking, call (423) 933-6986.

Breakaway Outreach
P.O. Box 3452
Cleveland, TN 37320

www.breakawayoutreach.com

Endnotes

[i] Maxwell, John. *Put Your Dream to the Test*. Thomas Nelson, 2009.

[ii] Maxwell, John. *Running with the giants: what Old Testament heroes want you to know about life and leadership*. Warner Books, 2002.

[iii] Eldredge, John. *The Sacred Romance*. Thomas Nelson, 1997.

[iv] Chan, Francis. *Crazy Love*. David C. Cook, 2008.

[v] Tozer, A.W. *The Pursuit of God*. Christian Publications, 1982.

[vi] Bonhoeffer, Dietrich. *The Cost of Discipleship*. Macmillan, 1979.

[vii] Barnett, Matthew. *The Cause Within You*. Tyndale, 2011.

[viii] Eldredge, John. *Wild at Heart*. Thomas Nelson, 2001.

[ix] Smith, David. *The Life and Letters of St. Paul*. Hodder and Stoughton, 1919

[x] Knox, John. *Philemon Among the Letters of Paul*. University of Chicago Press, 1935

Printed in Poland
by Amazon Fulfillment
Poland Sp. z o.o., Wrocław